Don't Speed. READ!

Michael F. Opitz

SCHOLASTIC

NEW YORK • TORONTO • LONDON • AUCKLAND • SYDNEY
MEXICO CITY • NEW DELHI • HONG KONG • BUENOS AIRES

For Sheryl
This is what I did about it!

Acknowledgments

I am greatly indebted to all who helped me bring this book to fruition. I thank Lois Bridges, editor, for believing in my ability to write this book, for teaching me how to be a writer, and for her keen insights about teaching, learning, and friendship; Dr. David Freeman of the University of Texas at Brownsville, for helping me to better understand that there is more than one way to cross a bridge; Dr. Yvonne Freeman of the University of Texas at Brownsville, Dr. Roger Eldridge of Rhode Island College, and Dr. Valarie Lee of Rowan University, for their insights about fluency and for listening and responding to my ideas; Dr. Michael Ford, University of Wisconsin, Oshkosh, for his co-authorship on professional writings cited in this text; Lynn Perrich, fifth-grade teacher, for the many fluency discussions and for reviewing and responding to the initial framework on which this book is based; Roland Schendel, research assistant, for help with tracking down references, reading and responding to all drafts, and compiling the fluency activities in Appendix B; I would also like to thank the many individuals at Scholastic, who have helped us to shape this book, including Sarah Longhi, Ray Coutu, and Amy Rowe, and a special thank-you to Erich Strom, the copy editor who brought greater clarity to this book.

Cover design: Maria Lilja
Interior design: Melinda Belter
Editor: Lois Bridges
Production Editor: Sarah Longhi
Copy Editor: Erich Strom
ISBN-13 978-0-439-92650-8
ISBN-10 0-439-92650-5

Contents

Introduction

I stand before an eager group of teachers who want to know how they can use oral reading in meaningful ways to facilitate the reading growth of their students. As with other workshops I conduct, I fall into my familiar routine of generating questions from participants, writing each on an overhead transparency, anticipating that I will be able to structure the day around their questions. I am relaxed and take comfort in knowing that I am prepared.

But today proves different. Although the title of the workshop is Meaningful Ways to Use Oral Reading, reading fluency takes center stage. One by one, their questions emerge:

"Should children be placed in summer school based on their reading fluency scores?"

"How should we assess reading fluency?"

"Can you give us a definition of reading fluency?"

"Is it true that reading fluency leads to comprehension or is it the other way around?"

"Is naming many letters within one minute a good indicator of a child's reading fluency?"

Clearly, teachers across the country are concerned and, perhaps, even confused about the role of fluency in successful reading.

This book is the result of taking a close look at fluency and exploring the many ideas I discovered in my effort to answer teachers' questions. I read professional articles, read what reading educators of past decades had to say, read current publications, talked with colleagues and anyone else whose attention I could capture, thought about my own teaching experiences as an elementary school teacher and reading specialist, and reflected on my own reading fluency. This research led to important discoveries about reading fluency that now form the content of this book. My aim is to bring greater understanding to the reading fluency craze that appears to be sweeping the nation, leaving many children and adults with misconceptions of what competent readers do when they engage with a variety of texts. You'll learn that reading fluency is but one piece of the reading process; additionally, you'll discover meaningful ways to think about and enhance children's reading fluency.

The book is framed as a series of 12 steps. The first four need to be read in order because they provide the foundation for the rest of the steps. Beyond these first four steps, read the remaining steps the same way you would climb any set of steps. If you're like me, you climb steps in different ways, depending on your purpose and energy level. Sometimes we take steps individually, pacing ourselves so that we will not be worn out when we reach the top, conserving some energy for what awaits our arrival. Other times we take two or more at a time. Regardless of the way you choose to read the steps, reading and absorbing them all will enable you to design smart and sensible fluency instruction.

For each step, I include accompanying charts and forms, where appropriate. I conclude each step by inviting you to reflect on how the information connects to your teaching. I also encourage you to discuss your ideas with colleagues. Your discussion is sure to lead to additional ideas—and potentially more questions!

Beyond the 12 steps, you'll find two appendices. Appendix A showcases assessment procedures and forms. You may reprint these pages for your classroom use. In Appendix B you'll find the 17 fluency activities that are highlighted in Step 5. I open this appendix with a grid that provides an overview of the possible group sizes for each activity.

One last point I wish to underscore is this: Throughout this book, I make every effort to show as much as tell you how to design smart and sensible fluency instruction, to scaffold your learning the same way we scaffold children's learning. Before asking you to think about and construct a response for each step, I first model *how* and explain *why* I do *what* I do. Clearly, I am not asking you to do anything that I have not done myself.

Writing this book helped me to better understand many questions that surround reading fluency. It also helped me to see that there are many unanswered questions that warrant further investigation. This investigation will take time, energy, and courage. Children deserve all three.

Define Fluency

Consider these children. They each have their own way of reading, regardless of whether they are reading silently or orally:

Michael reads a text as quickly as possible.

Sheryl reads a text paying close attention to every word to pronounce each one correctly.

Roland reads a text with expression.

Are any of them fluent readers? The answer depends on how you define reading fluency. If you think of reading fluency as reading quickly, then you would conclude that Michael is a fluent reader. If you believe that accuracy is important, then you would most likely conclude that Sheryl is a good reader. Then there's Roland. If you equate reading with expression with fluent reading, then you would agree that Roland is a fluent reader.

But what if you believe none of the above? What if you believe that fluency consists of reading with appropriate speed, accurate word reading, and prosody (i.e., reading with expression by using intonation, stress, tempo, and phrasing) for the sake of better understanding the text when reading silently and helping listeners comprehend when reading orally? You would conclude none of the three is fluent because not one of them is exhibiting all three components of reading fluency as you've defined it.

My point here is that the definition we choose influences both the assessment and instruction we provide students. It also guides us to or away from teaching strategies and commercially published instructional materials. For example, if you believe that fluency can be defined as speed, you would emphasize speed when teaching students about fluency and you would purchase programs that measure students' words per minute to track their progress. The more words read per minute, the greater the reading progress. If you believe that fluency consists of speed and accuracy, you would emphasize both in your instruction and be inclined to use programs that do the same. If you believe that speed, accuracy, and prosody are all parts of fluency, you would address all three in your instruction and use programs that emphasize all three. And finally, if you believe that comprehension is an important element, you would emphasize it as well. Being aware of your definition, then, is a good first step toward providing smart and sensible fluency instruction.

It seems so easy, doesn't it? So why isn't it? Reflecting on my own teaching experiences and my professional reading, leads me to think that there are three good reasons. First, as teachers we are too busy preparing to think about much else. We are in survival mode. All we know is that we want the children to grow as readers and we do what we think is best to enable this growth to happen. If someone were to ask us *why* we were doing *what* we were doing, more often than not we would not have a definitive answer. Instead, we might offer comments such as, "The children seem to do well with this activity" or "I've seen tremendous reading gains when I have children do this activity." Later on, if we take the time to think about the question, perhaps as we're driving home from school, we would be able to articulate why we do what we do.

Not only are we trying to survive the demands of the classroom, we are also trying to survive the numerous imposed mandates, which include new programs and their accompanying consultants, no recess breaks for children and teachers alike, and countless accountability measures, many of which do not even seem relevant to informing classroom instruction. Little time is left for actually thinking through the philosophical premises behind such mandates. Yet taking time to think about instruction is exactly what we need to do if we truly want to advance students' reading ability. Being aware of instructional practices and the goals behind them is one characteristic of teachers whose students demonstrate high achievement (Wharton-McDonald, Pressley, & Hampston, 1998).

A second reason that defining fluency can be difficult is that there are so many proposed definitions and so little consensus in the professional literature. Some define it as being able to read quickly, accurately, and with proper expression, as do the authors of the *Report of the National Reading Panel* (National Institute of Child Health and Human Development, 2000). Schwanenflugel, Kuhn, Strauss, and Morris (2006) note that "there is general agreement that fluent reading incorporates the ability to read quickly, accurately, and when oral reading is considered, with expression" (p. 496). So according to them, readers only read with expression when they read aloud; they do not use expression when reading silently. Still others include comprehension in the definition (Johns & Bergland, 2006; Pikulski, 2006). And finally, there are those such as Duffy (2003), who equate reading fluency with oral language. In his words, "Fluency, whether in oral or silent reading, is 'reading like you talk'" (p. 201).

To add to the confusion, some change their definition depending on the context. For example, when investigating repeated reading, Samuels (1979) defines fluency as being able to read with word recognition accuracy and speed. But in a discussion of his theory of automaticity (2006), he defines fluency as "the ability to decode and comprehend at the same time" (p. 39).

Another reason that defining fluency seems difficult is that some authors of professional publications use the word without explicitly defining it, leaving the reader to make some inferences about the proposed definition. For example, in a recent publication, Winn, Skinner, Oliver, Hale, and Ziegler (2006) note, "Fluent reading involves rapid and accurate reading" (p. 196). This statement leaves the reader to wonder what else might be involved in fluent reading and whether the authors are going to consider all that might be involved or only the two factors they mention. Further reading leads the reader to infer that the authors define fluent reading specifically as reading rapidly with accuracy.

The professional literature often leaves us with different ideas about what constitutes reading fluency. We become more confused instead of clearer. We feel left on our own to figure out for ourselves what it means to be a fluent reader and just how important, or not, fluency is to reading comprehension, the essence of reading. This is not all bad, for thinking through ideas leads to greater understanding. Wrestling with the different ideas about fluency, for example, helps you become more clear and purposeful. You know what you believe, and you can articulate your beliefs with supporting evidence from your own teaching experiences, your experiences as a reader, and professional readings. You exude confidence and professionalism.

Many times, it is our desire to be better teachers that sends us on a journey to better understand an instructional practice. In fact, my guess is that the reason you are reading this book right now is that you want to better understand the contributions that fluency might play in your quest to help your students become better readers. In terms of working through your understanding of reading fluency and coming to terms with a definition, think how valuable your newer knowledge is to the children you teach! You will be more likely to exhibit many of the characteristics associated with effective teachers, such as the ability to articulate the reasoning behind what you do (Pressley, Allington, Wharton-MacDonald, Block, & Morrow, 2001).

Taken a step further, imagine a school staff that takes the time to develop a definition of fluency to which they all subscribe so that all children across the grades will understand how fluency fits into reading and all other modes of language. Imagine, too, what the children who do not get this kind of coherent instruction must experience. Just after they have learned from one teacher that fast reading is what matters most, they hear comments from another teacher such as "Slow down! Good readers don't always read so quickly!" Children are left to themselves to puzzle out the importance of speed when reading. And some of them never do figure out how speed factors into reading, leaving them with grave misconceptions about what readers do in their everyday lives when they read many different kinds of texts.

Given all of this discussion about the importance of defining fluency, providing you with my definition seems appropriate. So what's my definition of reading fluency? As a result of my professional reading, my teaching experiences at many different grade

FIGURE 1.1

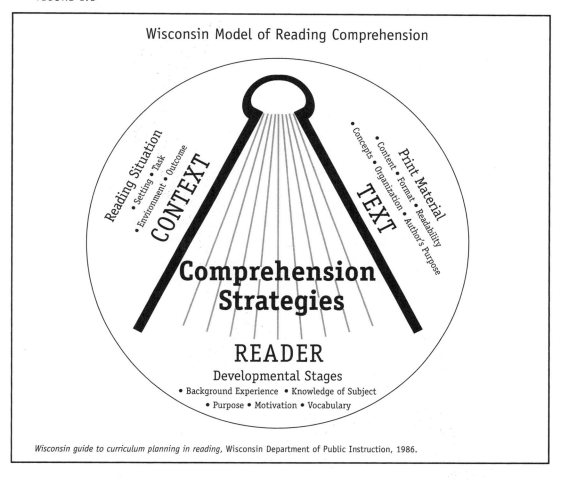

Wisconsin Model of Reading Comprehension

Reading Situation
• Setting • Task
• Environment • Outcome
CONTEXT

Print Material
• Content • Format • Readability
• Concepts • Organization • Author's Purpose
TEXT

Comprehension Strategies

READER
Developmental Stages
• Background Experience • Knowledge of Subject
• Purpose • Motivation • Vocabulary

Wisconsin guide to curriculum planning in reading, Wisconsin Department of Public Instruction, 1986.

levels, my experience as a parent, and my personal experiences with learning to read and how I now read, I see reading fluency as the ability to silently or orally read a text with appropriate speed, adjusting it as needed within a given text, with relative accuracy, and with appropriate phrasing, intonation, tempo, and expression (i.e., prosody). Fluency is a dynamic rather than static process. It fluctuates depending on factors such as the difficulty of the text, the topic of the text, the reading environment, and the reader's background for the text, interest in the text, and motivation. I agree with Samuels (2006) who notes, "Fluency is situational. This means that fluency is like happiness, in that we are not happy all the time, nor are we fluent all of the time" (p. 39). Figure 1.1 shows the many factors that contribute to successful reading and that impact fluency, a small part of the reading process.

What? No inclusion of comprehension in my definition? It's not a mistake; it is intentional. Comprehension is much more than speed, accuracy, and prosody, the three elements most often used to define reading fluency. Making comprehension an attribute of fluency would minimize its importance. Comprehension is the essence of reading rather than a subcategory of fluency. Can the development of speed, accuracy, and prosody enhance comprehension? There appears to be co-relational evidence to show that, yes, all three can enhance comprehension (see Kuhn & Stahl, 2000, for a review of these studies). But that's about all these elements can do. We know that these three elements are not required for reading comprehension because there are many readers who are able to read with comprehension yet read at a slow pace, do not read with 100 percent accuracy, and lack the elements of prosody. Likewise, there are those readers who can read with all three elements of fluency yet when asked what they have read can state little to nothing. Clearly, while we want to discuss fluency along with comprehension, we need to be careful that we do not oversimplify the interaction between fluency and comprehension. This interaction is anything but simple (Applegate, Quinn, & Applegate, 2004).

➡ REFLECTION ⇨

Now that you have read about reading fluency, how would you define it? What would you use as evidence to support your definition? You might find the chart below to be of some help in thinking through your definition. On the left side, list the attributes that you believe contribute to reading fluency. On the right side, list the supporting evidence. Finally, summarize the attributes to create your definition of reading fluency.

DEFINING FLUENCY

Attributes of Fluency	Supporting Evidence

Summary Statement (your definition of reading fluency)

Connect Your Definition of Fluency With Your View of Teaching Reading

How many ways can you cross a bridge? I can think of two. You can begin on one side or the other. Does the bridge look the same regardless of which direction you cross it? I suppose that depends on how strongly you feel about where your journey originates. When I was living in Juneau, Alaska, for instance, there was a bridge that spanned the Gastineau Channel, connecting Juneau to the city of Douglas. When approaching the bridge from the Juneau side, there was a sign that read, Juneau Bridge. When approaching the bridge from the Douglas side, the sign read, Douglas Bridge. And although some people referred to the bridge using one name or the other, still others referred to it as the Juneau-Douglas Bridge. Regardless of the name, the bridge served a function. It enabled transportation of various means to and from the two communities while at the same time permitting the many types of ships and boats to pass underneath it. And so it is with reading fluency. I have often heard and read that fluency is the bridge to comprehension (Johns & Bergland, 2006; Rasinski, 2006). The basic idea is that readers begin their journey by learning to decode words. Once they can do that automatically, they can then cross the fluency bridge (e.g., using speed, accuracy, and expression) arriving at comprehension, their final destination. Seen this way, fluency is the bridge between word identification, where the reader first uses text-based processes, and comprehension, which focuses on reader-based processes.

But as I suggest above, there is another way that readers can cross this bridge. Readers can begin with their own understandings of a text (i.e., its structure), and the topic and their prior knowledge to get an overall view of it. In other words, they can begin with reader-based rather than text-based processes. Seen this way, readers approach the bridge from the comprehension side. Their reading leads to identification of words. Miscue analysis research supports this view (Brown, Goodman, & Marek, 1996) as does more recent research. For instance, according to the results of the 2002 National Assessment of Educational Progress (NAEP), those students who read a passage with accuracy and appropriate pace appeared to better understand what they were reading, whether it was silent or oral. An equally important finding, however, is that many of those tested needed additional instruction in comprehension. How can this be if fluency is seen as a bridge to comprehension? And then in their fluency study, Schwanenflugel, et al. (2006) report, "At all grades, there was significant variance in children's reading comprehension *not* accounted for by fluency" (p. 519). Again, how can this be so if fluency is seen as a prerequisite to comprehension? Walczyk and Griffith-Ross (2007) propose compensatory-encoding theory (C-ET) to help answer this question. Briefly, the theory espouses that poor word readers use compensations such as slowing reading rate, pausing, and looking back to help automatic reading to succeed when reading [comprehension] fails. In their words, "According to C-ET, readers with poor word reading, small working memory capacities, or poor listening comprehension *can* [emphasis added] comprehend well . . ." (p. 563).

Does crossing the fluency bridge really have to be this linear? Can readers use both visual features of words (text-based) and background knowledge (reader-based) simultaneously to read with greater fluency? You bet they can, as the research findings on assisted rereading of texts suggest. For example, in the original repeated reading procedure reported by Samuels (2006), the teacher first read the text aloud while the students followed along. Doing so enabled students to hear that fluent reading sounds like talking. It's not too fast, too slow, or read in a monotone. Instead, the reader adjusts the speed as appropriate, and with prosody to best help listeners comprehend. Students were then permitted to read the text silently as many times as they needed in order to feel comfortable reading the text aloud. In other words, the students first used comprehension but they also had to use visual features (e.g., typographical cues) as they were practicing the text. Both their understanding of and responses to specific words helped them to sound fluent.

For more evidence that this is the way readers actually cross the bridge—which might seem like an indecisive traveler going back and forth—examine what you do to prepare a Read-Aloud for an interested audience. If you're like me, you first read through the entire text so that you can gain an understanding of it and ensure that you can pronounce all the words with ease. This understanding helps me see how I want and need to use my voice, when I should change my rate of reading as a way of conveying the intended meaning, and how I need to phrase the text so that I can make the read-aloud sound like natural speech. I can only make these decisions by taking a look at the typographical cues (e.g., end punctuation, punctuation used within a sentence, bold print, italic print, how the words are chunked together and the spaces between them). In other words, I have to use the visual features to better assist listeners comprehend the text. With all of this knowledge in place, I then practice the text a couple of times to bolster my confidence when reading before the group. As an aside, I also use the same process as a vocalist. When learning to sing an art song, regardless of the language, I first have to comprehend the lyrics and understand the intent of the song. Most often I need to hear an accomplished vocalist sing the song to assist my comprehension of it and how I should handle the song. Once understood, I can begin to practice paying attention to appropriate speeds (most songs require several), expression, and accuracy so that I can best communicate the message and emotion of the song.

What do these three ways of crossing a bridge have to do with your view of reading? In a word, everything! What I describe in the preceding narrative are three fundamental views of how we learn to read. The first, crossing from word identification to comprehension via fluency, is often called a bottom-up view of reading. Those that espouse this theory believe that there are specific stages readers go through on their way to becoming competent readers. They first concentrate on lower levels of information (e.g., letter identification) that are text-based and gradually progress to higher levels of information (e.g., comprehension), which is reader-based.

The second view, crossing from comprehension to word identification via fluency, is a top-down view of reading. Its advocates maintain just the opposite of the bottom-up folks. That is, they believe that readers first focus on the higher levels of information to better acquire the lower levels of information. Central to this view is the belief that readers bring a tremendous amount of background knowledge to a text, including knowledge of the topic, text, vocabulary, and letter-sound correspondences, and that they use all of this information when reading to make predictions about the text. The reader moves through the text with relative ease (e.g., appropriate speed, accuracy, and prosody) through a constant process of predicting, sampling, and confirming. However, when the reader's predictions about the text are inaccurate, he or she slows down to attend more closely to the text features.

The third view, crossing the bridge from comprehension to word identification, only to return to comprehension, is an interactive view of reading. People who extol this theory believe that readers use both higher-level and lower-level information to comprehend the text. In fact, they can use these processes simultaneously. They use background knowledge, meaning (semantics), word order (syntax), and phonics (graphophonics) in order to comprehend. Figure 2.1 shows these views.

At this point, the only question that might be at the front of your mind is "So what?" One good question deserves another so here's mine: Have you ever heard or read something that sounds right but feels wrong? Intuitively, the idea just doesn't seem quite right to you. I sure have! In fact, it was just such an incident that helped me to further understand the problem I was having with the current fluency craze that appears to be sweeping the nation—leaving many children behind to clean up the aftermath.

I was sitting in an auditorium listening to a speaker explain his views on reading fluency. At one point, the speaker commented, "Fluency is the gateway to comprehension!" His comment sounded right. It was also in line with some of what I had been reading about fluency. Yet, as had happened when I encountered this idea in my reading, it didn't feel right to me. And then it hit me! His statement and similar statements

FIGURE 2.1

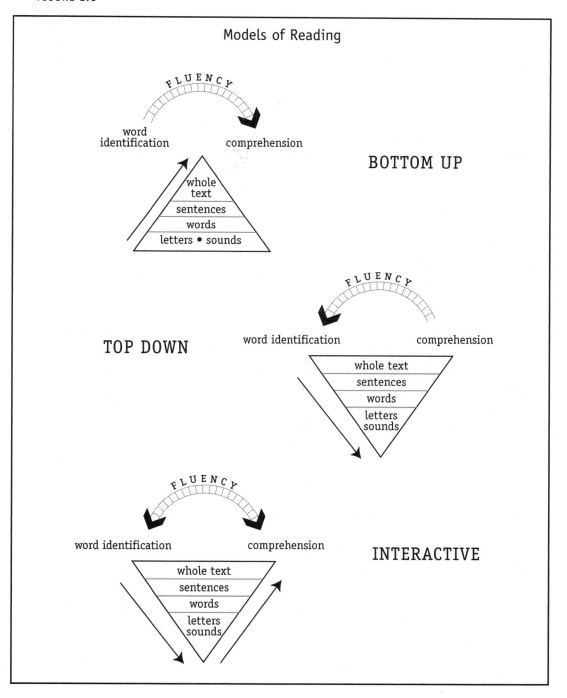

Models of Reading

FLUENCY

word identification   comprehension

BOTTOM UP

whole text
sentences
words
letters • sounds

FLUENCY

TOP DOWN   word identification   comprehension

whole text
sentences
words
letters sounds

FLUENCY

word identification   comprehension   **INTERACTIVE**

whole text
sentences
words
letters sounds

in the professional literature did not align with my view of teaching reading. This aha moment helped me to clarify not only why I was struggling with the whole "fluency as a prerequisite to comprehension" notion, but also how I approach assessing and teaching fluency. I came to realize that in order to maintain personal integrity, my definition of fluency and my view of teaching reading had to coincide.

And so it is with all of us as teachers. Although you may not be conscious of your view of reading, you can't escape it. It shows itself in your everyday teaching practices. It's like the Force; it is always with you. Quite honestly, I think having an unconscious belief is one reason that many are currently frustrated with what they are expected to do. Say you are a teacher who holds a top-down view of reading. As such, you believe that reading speed fluctuates depending on what the reader encounters within the text. At a staff meeting you are told that you need to document children's reading progress by measuring the number of words per minute (WPM) they can read. It is no small wonder that you would most certainly be frustrated if not irritated that you have to spend so much time assessing and tracking WPM. Yet because you cannot articulate your view of reading, you aren't fully aware of why you are so frustrated. All you can tell those who will listen to you is that it just isn't right to use WPM as an indicator of students' reading progress.

Those of you who teach kindergarten or first grade may be aware of developmentally appropriate practices as put forth by International Reading Association and the National Association for the Education of Young Children (1998). You would be inclined to believe in the importance of oral language as a foundation of reading in general and fluency in particular. That is, you would help children to first see how we use speed, accuracy, and prosody to best convey information when we talk with one another. You would also be interested in helping children to develop other critical early literacy components such as print concepts, phonological awareness, letter identification, the alphabetic principle, and story sense. You would not, however, see any need to give children timed tests to see how quickly they can name letters within a minute because this wouldn't matter to you. What would matter is the letters children know and don't know so that you can help them learn to identify all letters.

I hope you are still tuned in because here's the major point. Whether they are conscious or unconscious, beliefs guide your actions. However, there is ample evidence that you are more likely to maximize students' reading potential if you can articulate *why* you do *what* you do (Pressley et al., 2001). Being conscious of your beliefs puts you in a better position to select from the vast array of assessment and teaching strategies, as well as commercially prepared materials that relate to your view.

Knowing your view also helps you to better understand those that are not like yours. You can see how various views are alike and how they're different. Finally, knowing your view, and knowing other views as well, puts you in a better position to differentiate instruction. That is, as much as you might want to exclusively rely on your view, the children help you to see that you cannot always do so. Different children learn in different ways and knowing about several views enables you to use what works best for the children you teach. Indeed, you realize that the reading process is complex, and that there are no simple answers.

Here's the real clincher: We all want children to maximize their potential as readers. Being conscious of our view and our actions makes it possible to accomplish this huge task. We need to take some time to think about why we do what we do, which is the whole point of the following reflection.

➡ REFLECTION ⇒

Just what is your view of reading? How does it align with your definition of fluency? Write your ideas in the space provided below. Either before or after writing, place yourself on the continuum shown here and explain why you placed yourself in that spot.

← **Bottom-Up**   **Interactive**   **Top-Down** →

Your View of Reading:

Make Sure You Are Truly Assessing Reading Fluency

The thought of explaining reading fluency assessment led me to these two scenarios:

Scenario 1: Choral Singing
This is the moment the chorus and the soloists have been waiting for. They have rehearsed so that they can best communicate the music. Some of the selections require soloists, all of whom come from within the chorus. The soloists are positioned in the chorus so that when it is their turn to sing solo, they can step forward into the spotlight with ease. As each of them does so, the remainder of the chorus provides backup music, which greatly enhances the solo. Although the spotlight is on the soloist, the chorus and the soloist work together to convey the music's message. The soloist is part of the whole.

Scenario 2: Weightlifting
The weightlifter meets his coach at the gym. "So what muscle group should we work today?" asks the coach. The weightlifter responds, "Let's work the back." That decided, the coach takes the weightlifter through a series of exercises designed to work the back. Other muscles also have to engage to enable many of these exercises. For example, the arm and leg muscles have to engage as the weightlifter readies himself for the dead lift, one of several back exercises. The other muscles are there to support many of the moves, and work together to help the weightlifter develop the back muscles. The back muscles are part of the whole.

What's the point of these two scenarios? What do they have to do with assessing reading fluency? Just as the soloist and the chorus work together to communicate the message of the music, and the back muscles and the other secondary muscles work together to enable the weightlifter to perform, so, too, do fluency assessment and several other reading assessments work together to perform their task: revealing useful information about readers. We need to keep in mind that assessing fluency is only one part of a thorough reading assessment. It is part of the whole, nothing more and nothing less. Indeed, for many decades now, we have known that the only thing more complex than the reading process is the assessment of it (Strang, 1969). And as many of you know, useful assessment takes time. It is anything but quick and it is anything but dirty.

FIGURE 3.1

Relationship of Fluency Definition to Fluency Assessment

If your definition of fluency is	the focus of your assessment would be . . .
the ability to read at given rate,	reading speed.
the ability to read with accuracy,	word accuracy.
the ability to read with prosody,	prosody (e.g., expression, phrasing, and tone).
the ability to read at a given rate, identify words accurately, and read with prosody,	rate, accuracy, and prosody.
the ability to read at a given rate, identify words accurately, read with prosody, and comprehend,	rate, accuracy, prosody, and comprehension.

Without a doubt, assessing fluency is a necessary step for anyone who desires to deliver smart and sensible fluency instruction. As a result of interpreting readers' performances on any given assessment measure, we are in a better position to design appropriate instruction. In other words, assessment drives instruction.

But what should be assessed? How should it be assessed? In part, the answers to these two questions depend on your definition of fluency and your view of teaching reading in general and fluency in particular. (See Figure 3.1.) If you equate fluency with being able to read quickly, you will most likely assess reading speed. If you equate it with accuracy, you would be more inclined to assess for word accuracy. If you equate it with prosody, you would assess expression, phrasing, and intonation. If you believe all three are components of fluency, you would assess for all three. If you believe that comprehension is also a subcategory of fluency, you would assess all four. Clearly, as Samuels and Fargstrup (2006) note, "how one defines fluency influences how it will be measured" (p. 2).

In Step 1, I define reading fluency as the ability to silently or orally read a text with appropriate speed, adjusting it as needed within a given text, with relative accuracy, and with appropriate phrasing, intonation, tempo, and expression (i.e., prosody). Fluency is a dynamic rather than static process. It fluctuates depending on factors such as text difficulty, the topic of the text, the reading environment, and the reader's background for the text, interest in the text, and motivation. I also explain my reasoning for not including comprehension as a subcategory of reading fluency. To reiterate, I see comprehension as much more than speed, accuracy, and prosody, the three elements most often used to define reading fluency. To make it an attribute of fluency would minimize its importance. Comprehension is the essence of reading.

Likewise, many elementary-aged students I have taught, and those I continue to work with in my role as a literacy coach, reading professor, author, and consultant, have provided me with more than enough firsthand experiences to conclude that some children, even those who carry the "struggling reader" label, read with excellent comprehension but little fluency. In fact, some of these children are able to demonstrate higher-level comprehension skills such as inferring and evaluating yet have difficulty with lower-level comprehension skills such as identifying facts. I am not suggesting that fluency instruction be isolated from comprehension. My point is that comprehension can and does occur without fluency.

My definition of fluency aligns with my interactive view of reading (see Step 2 for an explanation of three ways to view reading). Consequently, I believe that to truly assess fluency, I need to first provide students with an overview of the selection. Doing so will enable them to use comprehension to better read with fluency. As Karp (1943) noted years ago, "Basic to reading with expression is reading with comprehension, which comes as a result of having an overview of, and an insight into, a passage of prose or poetry" (p. 103). I can accomplish this goal by reading the passage to students while they follow along silently. After a brief discussion of it, I then provide students with some practice time after which they read the passage orally to me. Using a rubric such as the one shown in Appendix A, I can then assess how they read the text in terms of the descriptors noted on the rubric.

As an alternative, I can provide students with some background for the passage and have them read it silently, perhaps even orally, to themselves so that they feel rehearsed, and therefore more at ease, when I assess their reading fluency. I agree with Betts (1946) who stated decades ago, "When initial reading is done silently, a higher degree of expression and fluency in oral reading may be achieved. The preliminary silent reading acquaints the pupil with material so that the oral rereading may bring out the mood and intent of the author" (pp. 500–501).

To be sure, because of my definition of fluency and my view of reading, I can see no purpose in assessing fluency with a "cold read" (i.e., a first encounter of the text). A cold read *would* help me to ascertain other important information, such as how students approach unfamiliar text, and what they do when they come to unknown words. But this is not why I am assessing students right now. I want to truly assess their fluency.

"But we've always done it that way!" you might be thinking. Actually, we have not. Although using a cold read is alive and well in the new millennium, it appears to have come about to save time (Brecht, 1977). Originally, Emmett Betts (1946), often credited with developing the informal reading inventory and the criteria that are used to determine children's independent, instructional, and frustration reading levels, promoted silent reading followed by an oral rereading. Given what we know about how readers interact with text, it seems logical to return to Betts's original procedure, which is standard when administering the Comprehensive Reading Inventory (2007). Indeed, the fluency lessons that appear to yield the greatest results are those that first provide the reader with an overview, often with the teacher reading aloud as the readers follow along reading to themselves (Kuhn & Stahl, 2000).

Beyond this explanation, though, I feel compelled to ask, "So what if you've always done it that way?" We continue to learn more about how children acquire reading. We have to remember that we still do not know with certainty how individuals learn to read. We have many ideas but the children themselves serve as good reminders that we still have some learning to do. Many reading researchers interested in understanding fluency also help us to see that there are still many unanswered questions. In short, our job is not to serve a "fluency orthodoxy" but to serve children.

And in case you are wondering, let me put your mind at ease. I am well aware of some standardized fluency measures that are currently in use (e.g., DIBELS). Because they are not aligned with my definition of fluency and because I am trying to show you as much as tell you about how to align your definition with the assessment(s) you use, I do not discuss them at length. I can find little reason, for instance, in using words read correctly per minute (WCPM) as a measure of children's reading growth. Yes, I am aware of the grade-level norms as cited by researchers such as Harris and Sipay (1990), Blachowicz, Sullivan and Cieply (2001), Hasbrouck and Tindal (2006), and Allington (2006). I am also aware that many teachers are using WCPM because of recent mandates stemming from the Reading First initiative, a part of the No Child Left Behind legislation. And, yes, I know that WCPM is promoted in some of the teaching resources aimed at helping teachers better assess fluency (e.g., *3-Minute Reading Assessments*, Rasinski and Padak, 2004). WCPM is also a part of some fluency activities aimed at helping children to improve their reading speed (e.g., repeated reading).

Knowing all of this information about WCPM puts me in a better position to state why I do *not* see it as helpful information in assessing reading. First, as Allington (2006) and others (Flurkey, 2006; Goodman, 2006; Harris & Sipay, 1990; Hiebert, 2006; Pressley, Hilden, & Shankland, 2005) explain, there are many factors that can and do affect reading rate. Ten of these factors are listed in Figure 3.2.

Second, as an elementary school teacher and a reading specialist, I rarely if ever used WCPM. Did I make you gasp? I didn't mean to! This is not to say that I did not pay attention to reading rate or see the value in it. Quite the contrary. It is because I

FIGURE 3.2

Ten Factors That Can Affect Reading Rate

Factor	Brief Explanation
• Understanding that reading must make sense	Those children who monitor themselves in a timed reading are often penalized because they take time to self-correct when they realize they have deviated from the text. Self-correction takes time, therefore they do not get as far in the passage, or on a list, if a list of words is used.
• Purpose and desire	Sometimes students are assessed on a text but have no purpose for reading it. Likewise, motivation plays a critical role in all areas of reading, fluency included (Walczyk & Griffith-Ross, 2007).
• Lack of background for the passage	Background knowledge of a text makes reading it much easier, and often much faster.
• Text difficulty	As noted by several researchers, such as Hiebert (2006), text matters when assessing fluency. It needs to be at an appropriate level. And, as Harris and Sipay (1990) note, "Norms for reading rate can be misleading because they vary considerably with the nature of the material" (p. 633).
• The environment	Students can feel threatened and uncomfortable if they sense that the environment is unsafe. Likewise, some children are unable to block out background noise. I, for one, have much difficulty reading in a room with a ticking clock.
• Audience	Students read differently for different audiences.
• Self-confidence	Lack of self-confidence can show itself when students are being assessed. They appear hesitant. This can be seen when they are required to do a cold read.
• Individual style	Some individuals simply process information more slowly than others (Harris & Sipay, 1990; Pressley, Gaskins, & Fingeret, 2006). Their slower processing is not necessarily a sign of a learning problem but may reflect individual differences.
• Inability to apply phonics skills to decode unknown words	There are many levels of knowing. Being able to do isolated phonics activities is no guarantee that students will be able to transfer these skills to reading connected text.
• Limited sight vocabulary	Durkin (1990) noted that there is a written context only if the reader can read most of the words. Readers need to have a store of words that they can identify instantaneously.

saw (and still see) just how valuable rate can be that I wanted to use it in appropriate ways. What I found (and still find) most valuable about reading rate is showing children how readers speed up and slow down within and across a variety of texts to best show their interpretation and understanding of the texts, and that it is natural to do so (Flurkey, 2006). I want them to understand how they can use rate to keep an audience interested in what they are reading. I can also see using reading rate to compare silent and oral reading to determine who might need help with understanding how to read silently. In the intermediate grades especially, students' silent reading rate should be higher because each word does not need to be vocalized. The same rate score for silent and oral reading could be an indication that the reader is subvocalizing. This being said, we have to use the results with caution. As Harris and Sipay (1990) note, "The rate at which pupils read under test conditions may not be the same as the rate that they employ in their daily reading in school" (p. 633). So, yes, reading rate can be important but for more complex reasons than WCPM advocates would have us believe.

Third, most often WCPM administration procedures call on students to do a timed, cold read of a passage. After doing specified calculations, the score is recorded. Students often do a second timed reading of the same text—and guess what? Their WCPM increases! I can make little sense of the wonder that is often expressed when this occurs. It seems so obvious to me that the WCPM would naturally increase because the child now has an understanding of the text and has seen it once before. He has had some time to practice it.

Fourth, students often mirror our behaviors. It should come as no surprise that students see good reading as fast reading when they are assessed and taught in this manner. What continues to surprise me, though, is when educators who use WCPM for assessment and timed readings in their instruction make comments such as "I just don't understand why they read so quickly. They are not even paying attention to what they are reading!" I, for one, do not want to be found guilty of contributing to children's misunderstandings of reading. I want them to understand from the very beginning that reading is about making sense and that reading rate can be useful as a comprehension tool.

Finally, like many of you, I was in school in the 1960s, when reading speed was seen as an important goal. Like many of you, I had well-meaning teachers who used the machines that would flash either phrases or sentences at a given rate in an effort to make us faster readers. It didn't appear to work, as a recent speaking engagement helped me to see. I provided the teachers, many of whom were my age, with time to read the same text silently. Guess what? They finished reading at different times. It seems to me that we should accept this variation as a difference rather than a deficiency. We all process text at different rates and this variation is natural.

With my fluency definition and view of teaching reading in place, I am now able to address what should be assessed and why. I can now ask and answer three important assessment questions:

- What do I want to know?

- Why do I want to know it?

- What assessment technique can I use to discover this information?

In Figure 3.3, I show how I answer these questions. Specific administration procedures and sample forms are available in Appendix A.

As you can see, a thorough assessment of reading fluency can be pretty involved. Fortunately, most of the assessment tools can easily be integrated within existing classroom routines. The independent reading record, for example, is already used during independent reading time. We can never get away from observation, can we? However, what I suggest is to use just one observation question as a focal point for any given day and keep a record of what you notice for each student for that one question only (see Appendix A for a form designed for this purpose). This observation can be completed at various times during the day as students are reading in many different content areas. Even though assessment is involved, it can be done quickly because you already have the structure in place and you know exactly what it is you are trying to assess. But, as with reading, quick or slow is not what the assessment is about. The primary objective is to discover what it is that students know so that we can use it to help them learn what they need to know.

Regardless of the fluency measure we use, we need to make sure that we are looking at comprehension as well—children need to know that comprehension matters. Consequently, some type of comprehension assessment accompanies nearly every assessment technique I suggest.

What if your definition of fluency is different from mine? As I see it, you have a couple of options. You can use parts of what I offer here. For example, you might believe that the main point of fluency is accuracy. Consequently, you may decide to use the running record as a way of documenting accuracy. Second, you can search out other references that support your view.

No question about it: A necessary step in delivering smart and sensible fluency instruction is aligning your assessment techniques with your fluency definition and view of reading. Taking the time to do so will go a long way in helping you to make sense of the *why* behind the *what*. Just imagine how confident you will feel as a result of being able to articulate your ideas!

FIGURE 3.3

The What, Why, and How of Fluency Assessments

What do I want to know?	Why do I want to know it?	Which assessment technique(s) will best help me discover this information?*
Do students understand how to vary their reading rate within and across texts?	• Adjusting reading rate to purpose is one hallmark of a proficient reader. I want to know whether students understand the importance of speeding up and slowing down within and across texts as a tool for understanding. • Some students may have the misperception that good reading means fast reading. I want to identify these students so that I can help them to better understand how to use rate of reading as a tool for understanding.	• Observation • Student self-report (Step 4, pages 27–32.)
To what degree do students read with accuracy?	• Being able to identify words accurately and instantaneously can facilitate students' reading fluency. I need to discover whether they are able to do both so that I can help those children in need. • Some students may have the misunderstanding that they must identify every word with 100 percent accuracy, and that could be retarding their reading growth. I need to help these students understand that readers rarely read with 100 percent accuracy. Instead, they focus on the understanding of the text.	• Running record • Modified miscue
Do students understand how to use prosody when reading?	• Reading with expression, in meaningful phrases with attention to typographical cues, facilitates comprehension. All three can help students better interpret the meaning of the text. • Proficient readers chunk what they read rather than process word by word. I want to make sure students understand how to chunk.	• Holistic Oral Reading Fluency Scale (NAEP) • Observation
How much time do students spend reading?	• Much reading is one way for students to develop a large vocabulary and thus read with more fluency, both silently and orally. I want to make sure that all students are given enough time to read in school, especially if they are not able to read after school for one reason or another. I also want to provide easy access to all kinds of texts, attractive books included.	• Independent reading record • Observation

* Note: Unless otherwise noted, procedures and sample forms for the assessment techniques listed are provided in Appendix A.

REFLECTION

Think about your definition of fluency, your view of teaching reading, and the fluency assessment measures you have read about. Use the chart below to write your definition, view of reading, and the assessment measures you currently use so that you can see firsthand how they relate to one another. Are there discrepancies? Are there techniques you would consider adding to your assessment toolbox?

ARE YOU IN ALIGNMENT?

My Definition of Fluency	My View of Teaching Reading	Fluency assessment Techniques

Allow Students to Self-Assess

"No! You just don't understand!" he said in between sobs.

"You're right. I don't. Please tell me so that I do."

And that's when third-grade student John told me something he knew about himself that only he could state. Here's how the sharing came about:

> I was working with third graders who were reading *The Chocolate Touch* (Catling, 1952). I had rounded up enough hard- and soft-cover copies, so that each student could have his or her own copy. When John didn't get a hardcover copy, he started crying, saying that he could not read the soft-cover copy I had given him. I assured him that he could and showed him that the first pages of both versions were the same. In between deep sobs, he told me, "No! You just don't understand!" I replied, "You're right. I don't. Please tell me so that I do." He took both books and, pointing to the page in the hardcover copy, noted that there was more space around the words and that the paper was thicker. That was why he needed the hardcover version. It was easier on his eyes.

Tapping students' knowledge about themselves to better understand their perspective is such a simple yet often overlooked valuable assessment resource. As John showed me, students can be informants on their own learning. He had assessed himself and he knew what he needed. Had I not asked John to explain, I would have been left to my own reasoning to puzzle out why he responded the way he did. Clearly, "students seldom fail to show considerable insight" (Strang, 1969, p. 81).

You might think it peculiar that student self-assessment is a stand-alone step rather than part of the assessment process described in Step 3. Usually it is included as one of several assessment techniques to consider for a thorough reading assessment. The problem is that there is so much to know about different assessment techniques that student self-assessment sometimes gets lost. It is viewed as an option rather than a necessity.

Especially as it pertains to reading fluency, student self-assessment is anything but an option. It is critical. Why, you ask? First, when students assess themselves, they are more apt to understand what they are learning and how they are progressing toward their goals.

If you want students to focus on all three areas of reading fluency (speed, accuracy,

FIGURE 4.1

Student Self-Evaluation of Reading Fluency Components

Name _____ Date_____

Title of text _____ Pages read_____

Now that you have finished listening to yourself read, read each of these statements and place a check in the appropriate column.

Statement	1 I need to keep working on this.	2 I did pretty well.	3 I did very well.
1. I read with just the right speed. I also slowed down or read more quickly to best help listeners understand the text.			
2. I read most words the way they were printed. Even if I missed a word, I kept reading if I knew that my missing it would not stop the listener from understanding.			
3. My reading sounded as if I was talking with a friend. It sounded natural.			

and prosody) during oral reading, you might have them use a self-evaluation rubric such as the one shown in Figure 4.1.

If students are focusing on learning how to adjust reading rate to meet their purpose when reading silently, for instance, they can call this purpose into mind before and while reading a text. Once finished reading, they can reflect on how well they met their goal using a rating scale or checklist such as the one shown in Figure 4.2.

Regardless, I have found that students need to be taught how to use these forms in order to get the most out of them. I recommend following the procedures in Figure 4.3.

Rather than use a rating form, you might have students reflect and write their thoughts in a reflection log. To get students to think about how they can use rate as a reading tool, you might have them record the title of the selection, the number of pages

FIGURE 4.2

Student Checklist for Adjusting Rate to Purpose

Name _____ Date_____

Title of text _____ Pages read_____

1. I set a purpose for reading. ❑ Yes ❑ No

2. I thought about what I already knew about this topic. ❑ Yes ❑ No

3. I changed my speed of reading when I needed to so that
   I could best understand the text. ❑ Yes ❑ No

---

read, and the amount of time it took to read them. Students could then estimate how much time it might take to complete the reading, assuming that the text will span several reading sessions.

Seen this way, rate can be an excellent study strategy for students in the upper elementary grades. It can help them better understand how to allot the time they'll need to study a given text. It can also show them how the various factors related to fluency, such as their background for the topic, their interest in the topic, and the type of text, all impact their rate of reading. It leaves them with an understanding of the way readers use reading rate in their everyday lives.

What's that? You say that your students need a little more structure for their reflection logs? If so, you might consider using a form similar to the one shown here in Figure 4.4.

Another reason for using self-assessment is that it helps students see that assessment is not necessarily something that is done *to* them but rather *by* them in an effort to better understand themselves. In terms of reading fluency, then, if students are provided with an opportunity to talk about their perceptions of what constitutes a good reader, they become self-aware and as a result are in a better position to either keep or modify those perceptions. Change begins with awareness.

We can informally talk with students either as a group or individually about the characteristics of good readers, noting what they have to say on some sort of anecdotal record, such as the one I show in Figure 4.5. These characteristics relate to elements of

FIGURE 4.3

Teaching Procedures

Teaching Procedure for Self-Evaluation Rubric: Oral Reading (Figure 4.1)

- Set the focus. Ask:
  - Why might reading aloud with ease be important?
  - When might you use oral reading to communicate with others?
  - What might you want to listen for?

- Provide student with form and explanation. Tell the student:
  - Select a passage from a book or another text you are reading.

- Read the statements on the form.
  - Using a cassette tape and recorder, record your reading.
  - Rewind the tape and listen to yourself read.
  - Complete the form.

- Schedule time to meet with students individually.
  - Instruct student to bring his or her recording and completed form to you.
  - Listen to the tape.
  - Ask student to explain his or her self-evaluation.
  - Ask student to set a goal for the next reading.

Teaching Procedure for Self-Evaluation Checklist: Silent Reading (Figure 4.2)

- Set the focus. Ask:
  - Why might setting a purpose for reading be important?
  - Why is it a good idea to think about what you might already know?
  - When might you speed up or slow down when reading to yourself?

- Provide the student with form and explanation. Tell the student:
  - Select a passage from a book or another text you are reading.
  - Read the statements on the form.
  - Silently read your text.
  - Complete the form.

- Schedule time to meet with students individually.
  - Instruct the student to bring his or her completed form to you.
  - Ask student to explain his or her self-evaluation.
  - Ask the student to set a goal for the next reading.

FIGURE 4.4

Sample Reflection Log Form

Name _____ Date_____

Title of text _____

Number of pages read: _____ Number of minutes: _____

Based on today's reading, how long do you think it will take you to finish this text?

_____

_____

_____

_____

_____

_____

---

reading fluency as discussed in Step 1. The conversation might begin with questions such as these:

- What do you think makes someone a good reader?

- Do you read every text at the same pace?

- When you are reading, do you think that you need to state every word exactly as the author shows it?

- When you are reading aloud to a group, how do you use your voice? Why do you use it that way?

As you can see, student self-assessment can add much needed information for student and teacher alike. For it to be truly effective, though, we need to believe that students have something of value to say—that they can be informants on their own learning.

FIGURE 4.5

Anecdotal Record

Class responses to questions pertaining to reading fluency

Date: _____

Question(s) asked:

_____

_____

Student's name   Student's responses

_____   _____

_____   _____

_____   _____

_____   _____

_____   _____

_____   _____

_____   _____

_____   _____

_____   _____

_____   _____

_____   _____

_____   _____

_____   _____

REFLECTION

There are several additional ways that students can be informants on their own learning. I have listed these in the table below. Think about each one and how you might be able to use it in relationship to reading fluency.

STUDENT SELF-ASSESSMENTS

Self-Assessment Technique	How It Might Be Used to Assess Reading Fluency
Questionnaire	
Interest inventory	
Contributions to discussions	
Sharing information	
Various forms of writing: (journals, reflections, checklists)	

Use a Wide Array of Meaningful Reading Activities

Ask accomplished singers how they can sing well and they'll tell you: meaningful practice. Ask accomplished athletes how they can perform with what looks like ease and they'll tell you: meaningful practice. You get the idea. Meaningful practice is the foundation for accomplishing activities that matter to us.

The same can be said of reading fluency. As a result of meaningful practice, students' reading fluency is enhanced. But how do students get this meaningful practice? Perhaps one of the best ways to begin this meaningful practice from the start of schooling, if not before at home, is to provide children with a language-rich environment, one that encourages and supports their use of language in a variety of ways. Brian Cambourne's conditions of learning are useful here (see Figure 5.1). They provide children with opportunities to use language in a variety of ways. Consider two kindergarten students who talk with one another about a topic of interest. They can't help but use all aspects of fluency (speed, accuracy, and prosody) as they speak. Using these elements of language is natural, even though students might not be conscious that they are doing so. And what about the dramatic play that engages so many children? How can they not use prosody as they take on the personality that their role calls for?

Then, too, thanks to the work of Michael Halliday (1975), we know that children who have been immersed in a language-rich environment are flexible language users. That is, they use language in seven different ways. Knowing about these functions puts us in a better position to teach children who appear to be limited language users to become more flexible. Most important to the present discussion, by using oral language in these different ways, children also begin to learn about the elements of fluency. Figure 5.2 lists Halliday's functions and provides related sample activities that are sure to use all aspects of fluency.

By first creating the necessary conditions for using language, and then showing students how to use language in a variety of ways, we are providing them with an excellent start for understanding how fluency is a necessary part of communication, oral and written alike. Oral language sets the stage for helping children make the connection to the written word. When teaching children about using appropriate speed when they're reading, for example, we can call on their experiences with what they do to make themselves understood when they talk with one another. We can then proceed to explain that the same process applies to reading.

FIGURE 5.1

Cambourne's Conditions of Learning

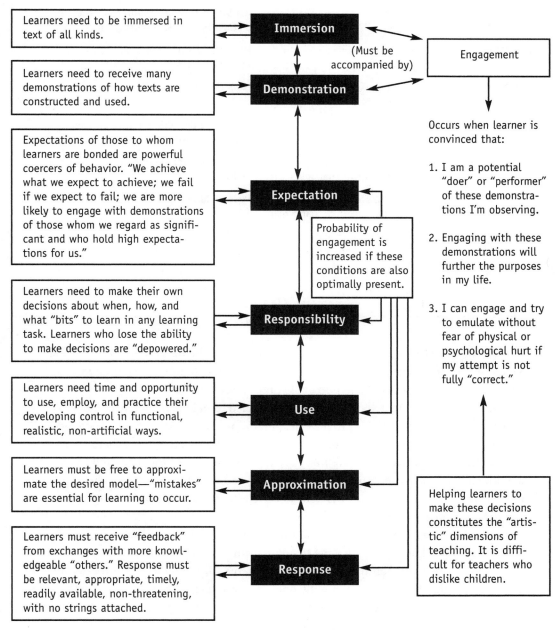

Source: Cambourne, B. (1995, November). Toward an educationally relevant theory of literacy teaching: Twenty years of inquiry. *The Reading Teacher, 49*(3): 182-202. Reprinted with permission of the International Reading Association.

FIGURE 5.2

Halliday's Functions of Language and Related Fluency Activities

Function of Language	Use	Activities that incorporate all aspects of fluency (speed, accuracy, prosody)
Instrumental ("I want.")	To satisfy needs or desires	Have children provide oral directions for others.
Regulatory ("Do as I tell you!")	To control the behavior of others	Have children play follow the leader.
Interactional ("Do as I tell you!")	To establish and keep relationships	Have children work together to plan a project or construct an object.
Personal ("Here I come!")	To express one's personal feelings or thoughts	Provide time for children to talk with one another.
Heuristic ("Tell me why.")	To discover and find out why something happens	Have children conduct simple experiments.
Imaginative ("Let's pretend.")	To create an imaginative world of one's own	Provide puppets and a dress-up center and provide time for children to use both.
Informative ("I have something to tell you.")	To provide information to others	Provide time for children to share announcements.

Another way that we can provide students with meaningful practice is to provide plenty of time for silent reading. Silent reading is so important to developing reading fluency that I devote an entire step to explaining it (see Step 10).

Deliberate use of an activity specifically designed to heighten students' understanding of fluency is a third way to provide meaningful practice. And we are not at a loss for such activities. In fact, the problem is choosing the best from among them. This selection happens at two levels. We first have to decide which of the many published activities align with our definition of fluency and reading. Then we choose the specific activity we want to use. I have found this to be relatively easy if I first identify what it is that I want students to learn about fluency.

These two selection levels identified, I have some good news and what you might consider some bad news. I'm guessing that you want the bad news first, that you want to save the best for last. Not to disappoint, then, here's the bad news. I cannot do the level two selection for you as you are the one who knows your students. You are the one who has completed the assessment and determined what students know and what they need to learn.

The good news is that I can show you a vast array of fluency activities that you can use, which is exactly what the following section is all about. To choose these activities, I followed my advice to you. I selected only those that align with my definition of fluency and view of reading. With the help of research assistant Roland Schendel, I consulted numerous professional publications in my effort to provide you with meaningful activities. Those shown here are drawn from Allington (2006), Johns & Berglund (2006), Kuhn & Stahl (2000), Opitz (1998), Opitz & Rasinski (1998), and Samuels & Fargstrup (2006). It was this research that led to another aha! for me. I had never considered which fluency activities might be considered "unassisted" (those that build on independent learning via independent practice) or "assisted" (those that model fluent reading behaviors to children, provide a wealth of print exposure, and emphasize practice to help enhance not only all areas of fluency, but comprehension as well). Kuhn and Stahl (2000) not only make this distinction clear, but they also point out that assisted activities are more effective at advancing reading fluency than unassisted activities. Given this finding, emphasizing assisted fluency activities makes good sense.

Another reason for using assisted activities is that social interaction is a big part of any language-rich classroom. It is this interaction that helps students better see the purpose for fluent reading, especially when they are sharing aloud.

Finally, a good reason for using assisted activities is that the majority of them begin with comprehension and then proceed to fluency. The activities give students some kind of overview, such as the teacher reading the entire text while students listen and follow along. Discussion then follows this reading. Then, and only then, do students practice the text in whole or part with a focus on fluency.

The common thread that ties all of these assisted fluency activities together is the repeated reading of the text. In all of the activities, students read the text at least three times. In Figure 5.3, I list the activities and provide a brief description. A detailed explanation of each activity is provided in Appendix B, thanks again to the efforts of my research assistant, Roland Schendel.

And, I have more good news. I thought it might be helpful for you to know which grouping structures relate to the different fluency activities I showcase in this text. Figure 5.4 will show you which grouping size you need for each given fluency activity. A bullet in the combination column indicates that the activity calls for more than one group size within a lesson. Some of these call for whole-class grouping, whereas others are done in small groups, with partners, or individually.

In *Reaching Readers* (Heinemann, 2001), Michael Ford and I provide a chart that describes these different group sizes, their advantages and disadvantages, and the appropriate use for each grouping structure. I include that chart here (Figure 5.5) because it can remind you of what to consider as you plan a given fluency activity.

FIGURE 5.3

Fluency Activities and Brief Descriptions

Name of Activity	Brief Description
Shared Book Experience (SBE)	Students are seated in front of a big book. After a focused introduction and a first read by the teacher, students chime in on a second reading.
Echo Reading	The teacher reads aloud a segment of text while students follow along. Then, in unison, students reread the same segment.
Choral Reading	Students read a text in unison.
Oral Recitation Lesson	The teacher reads aloud while students follow along. After discussing the text, the teacher then rereads the text, stopping at logical places, and students echo back each section of text. Students then read a portion of the text on their own until they feel comfortable with the text. They then read it to others in the group.
Fluency-Oriented Reading Lesson	Students read a grade-level text after the teacher first reads the text aloud and leads a discussion of the text. Students then practice reading the text in and out of school and read their part of the text to a partner the following day.
Read-Aloud	The teacher selects and practices a book to read aloud with specific emphases in mind.
Partner Reading	In some manner, students are paired and they read a text together. There are many variations of this procedure as described in Appendix B.
Readers Theater	Students rehearse a script and once the group feels prepared, present the play to the class, scripts in hand.
Cross-Age Reading	Students of different ages are paired for reading. They then read the same text.
Poetry Club	After hearing the teacher read some poetry and explain why he or she chose these poems to read aloud, students select their own poems and after practicing, read them aloud to an interested audience.
Read Around	Students gather around a table. In turn, they state the title of their book, provide a brief overview, and read a selected portion aloud to the group.
Guess the Emotion	Students read selected sentences expressively; their peers guess the target emotion.
Cut Apart	A story is cut up into sections, one section for each class member. After practicing, students read the sections in sequence.
Say It Like the Character	Students read a section of narrative text to themselves and decide how the character would actually say the words if he or she were present. Students then read the part aloud trying to sound just like the character.
Neurological Impress	The teacher sits alongside the student and reads into the student's ear while the student also reads aloud.
Reading While Listening	Students read silently while listening to a proficient reader read the text aloud. There are many variations to this procedure as described in Appendix B.
Closed-Captioned Television	The sound is turned off and the captions are turned on. Students then watch and read a given television show.

FIGURE 5.4

Fluency Activities and Group Sizes

Activity	Whole Class	Small Group	Partner	Individual	Comb.
Shared Book Experience (SBE)	•				
Echo Reading	•	•			
Choral Reading	•	•			
Oral Recitation Lesson	•			•	•
Fluency-Oriented Reading Lesson	•		•	•	•
Read-Aloud	•				
Partner Reading			•		
Readers Theater		•		•	•
Cross-Age Reading			•		
Poetry Club	•	•		•	•
Read Around		•			
Guess the Emotion	•	•			
Cut Apart	•	•		•	•
Say It Like the Character	•	•		•	•
Neurological Impress				•	
Reading While Listening	•	•	•		
Closed-Captioned Television	•	•			

Thinking through these considerations is sure to lead to greater success for both you and students.

So there you have them: a number of fluency activities to get you started or keep you going. Just which activity you use for any given lesson will depend upon your definition of fluency and view of reading. Your selection also depends on your knowledge of what students know and need to know which is drawn from your interpretation and use of fluency assessments.

Make no mistake: I realize that some or all of the activities I show here will be familiar to some of you. You may have used them for years or have heard of them but have yet to try them for one reason or another. And there's no question that the list is

Figure 5.5

Planning for Different Group Sizes

Group Size	Description	Advantages	Disadvantages	When It Works
Whole Class	Teacher works with the whole class and everyone participates in similar activities. In one way or another, the same text is often read by all students.	• Whole-class instruction builds a community of learners. • It provides a common knowledge base for all.	• Differentiating instruction is more difficult. • Some students can get frustrated or bored depending on the level of instruction. • Students may not interact as planned.	• Different learners are considered when planning instruction. • All members of the class are provided with a similar experience.
Small Group	Groups of two to five students work together to accomplish a given task.	• Grouping provides for focused instruction. • It engages more learners. • Students learn to work with one another.	• Students may not interact. • Groups create a higher noise level. • Students might be grouped together for too long. • Student perceptions of group can be negative.	• Group membership changes on a regular basis. • Students are taught how to respond to one another.
Partners	Students are paired up with one another to read text in one or more ways.	• Pairs tend to stay focused. • Partner work enables relationships to develop. • It encourages independent learning so the teacher can help those who need it.	• One of the two students may become too dependent on the other. • One of the two may dominate.	• Partners are switched on a regular basis. • Procedures are clearly understood by both.
Individual	Students work by themselves and each often reads a different text.	• Independent work allows students to read at a comfortable level and develop their own understandings. • It enables teacher to evaluate individual progress to determine what students know and need to know.	• Instruction can be hard to organize. • Students may become distracted and/or lose focus. • There may be little sense of community.	• Reading is at the appropriate level. • Students understand procedures. • An effort is made to bring students back together as either a small or large group to discuss what they've learned.

Source: Adapted from Opitz, M. and Ford, M. (2001). *Reaching readers: Flexible and innovative strategies for guided reading.* Portsmouth, NH: Heinemann.

Don't Speed. READ!

incomplete. In other words, although I think I exhausted my research assistant, the list is not intended to be exhaustive. Remember that I've only included those that align with my definition of fluency and reading.

REFLECTION

How about you? Which of the activities discussed in this chapter align with your views? Which have you tried or would like to try? Take some time to reflect on these questions and write notes on the reflection guide. If you are working with colleagues, getting together to discuss your findings is sure to lead to even greater understandings.

FLUENCY ACTIVITIES

Activity	Comments

Use a Variety of Texts

It's a familiar daily routine. The lyrics to "Zip-a-Dee-Doo-Dah" are displayed on a chart large enough for all to see. The first graders sing with gusto as Sandy, their teacher, strums the melody on her guitar and one of the children points to the words on the song chart.

Across the hall, Randy and his second-grade students are chanting "In Time of Silver Rain," by Langston Hughes, a favorite poem they have seen many times. The class is divided into two groups so that each group can read a stanza. Both groups then read the last three lines of each stanza together.

In both classrooms, the children are learning about fluency in meaningful contexts. They experience firsthand the why and how of reading with speed, accuracy, and prosody.

But why choose song lyrics and poems? Indeed, why use the many different kinds of texts I showcase in this step for teaching fluency? Because we are teaching children to be readers rather than merely teaching them about fluency. In everyday life, we read many different types of texts. What we read depends on several factors, including interest and purpose, and we adjust speed, accuracy, and prosody accordingly. Using a variety of texts, we can show children how to use fluency to aid comprehension in different contexts.

Let's not be fooled, however. There are many complexities involved in using texts. These range from the oversimplification of leveling systems often imposed on texts to how text factors impact readers. (See Paris & Carpenter, 2004, and Opitz & Ford, 2006, for a thorough discussion of these factors.) My purpose in this step is to present the many types of texts that are available to you to teach fluency and to explain how each might be used most effectively.

This being said, I do think that the level of texts you offer children in your effort to help them develop reading fluency is one point that needs some attention. There are those who advocate that lots of easy reading will help children the most (Allington, 2006; Clay, 1983; Hiebert, 2006; Krashen, 2004). As Hiebert notes, "The texts should give students opportunity to read fluidly without having to grapple with the pronunciation and meaning of many rare multisyllabic, single-appearing words" (p. 222). Based on my teaching experiences and experiences as a reader myself, I agree.

Nonetheless, there are others who note that children, with support from their teacher, can make gains reading more difficult text (Kuhn & Stahl, 2000). Much depends on the amount of support that the teacher provides. Clay (1991) provides spe-

FIGURE 6.1

Texts for Reading Fluency and Their Connection to Fluency Activities

Text Type	Fluency Activities (See Step 5 and Appendix B)
Song texts	Echo Reading, Choral Reading
Poetry	Poetry Club, Choral Reading
Predictable books	Shared Book Experience (SBE), Read-Aloud
Information (nonfiction)	Reading While Listening, Read-Aloud
Multilevel literature	Partner Reading, Cross-Age Reading
Series books	Read Around, Guess the Emotion
Chapter books	Read Around, Say It Like the Character
Scripts	Readers Theater
Magazines	Partner Reading, Read-Aloud
Newspapers	Partner Reading, Read-Aloud
Cyber-texts	Read Around, Read-Aloud
Real-life texts	Cross-Age Reading, Read Around
Leveled books	Read Around, Partner Reading
Basal readers	Fluency Oral Reading Lesson, Cut Apart
Textbooks	Reading While Listening, Cut Apart

cific examples of different levels of support a teacher can provide readers when introducing them to a text. Again, based on my teaching experiences and experiences as a reader myself, I agree.

Taking both views into account, it seems reasonable to use both types of texts to help children with fluency. It seems to me that when increased fluency is the focus the majority of the texts are going to be easy for students to read. However, using more difficult texts with support at times promotes students' growth. I do not see this as an either/or issue. We can and should use both.

Properly matching the type of text and the level of difficulty with the fluency teaching activities from Step 5 should help provide the kind of support students need in order to read any given text. So not only do I list in Figure 6.1 15 different types of texts that can be used to develop fluency, I also match each text with some of the fluency activities mentioned in Step 5. Please keep in mind, however, that these matches are merely suggestions to get you started. Many of these activities can and should be used with a variety of different texts. Ultimately, your instructional purpose and the level of support you wish to provide will help you select both the text and the activity.

Following is additional information for each type of text that includes a description, examples, and reasons for using the text when teaching about fluency.

• Song Texts

DESCRIPTION: Song texts are just what you might think: familiar songs that have been made into picture books. Most often, the musical score is also included, as is a CD that features a singer singing the song with instrumental accompaniment.

EXAMPLES:
America the Beautiful by Katharine L. Bates
A-Tisket, a-Tasket by Ella Fitzgerald
Here We Go Round the Mulberry Bush by Will Hillenbrand
Don't Laugh At Me by Steve Seskin & Allen Shamblin
Skip to My Lou by Mary Ann Hoberman & Nadine Bernard Westcott

WHY USE THEM TO TEACH FLUENCY?
Singing is a part of most youngsters' everyday lives. Songs can help children make the transition from oral fluency to using fluency when reading. That is, many children have familiar favorites such as "Here We Go Round the Mulberry Bush" that they have memorized and can sing but cannot yet read on the page. Using their oral language as a strength, we can show children how these songs look in print. We can point out that the song needs to be sung with speed, accuracy, and prosody by actually pointing to the lyrics as children sing them and by using the musical scores or the CD. What better way, for example, to teach about phrasing than to use song lyrics? And how about speed? All songs are written with a tempo in mind. Sharing this with children is an excellent way to show rather than tell how readers use different speeds. And think about accuracy. The song lyrics have to be sung with a high degree of accuracy in order to understand the message of the song.

• Poetry Texts

DESCRIPTION: Poetry is writing in which rhythm, sound, and language are used to create images, thoughts, and emotional responses. Usually concise, poetry takes on many forms such as narrative poetry, which tells a story; lyric poetry, in which much rhythm is used; humorous poetry, which portrays everyday objects or events in absurd ways; and nonsense poetry, which uses meaningless words and much exaggeration (Goforth, 1998).

EXAMPLES:
In the Swim and *Handsprings* by Douglas Florian
School Supplies: A Book of Poems by Lee Bennett Hopkins
Block City by Robert Louis Stevenson
Down to the Sea in Ships by Philemon Sturges
When I Heard the Learn'd Astronomer by Walt Whitman

WHY USE IT FOR TEACHING FLUENCY?
I can think of few ways that are better for teaching students about all three aspects of fluency than poetry. It is a natural fit. For example, poems are written in phrases, making them ideal authentic texts for showing children why reading in phrases, one element of prosody, is useful. And what better way to teach about speed than to use a poem to show students how we can speed up and slow down within a text to create interest and understanding? And think about accuracy! Most poets economize on the words they use, making it a must to read every single one of them as written if we want to best understand the poet's intended meanings. Finally, because they are usually short, poems tend to be less intimidating for even the most novice reader.

• Predictable Books

DESCRIPTION: Predictable books are written with specific features that enable children to read with ease. These characteristics are as follows:

- *Pictures that support the text.* These pictures show what the text says, making it possible for the reader to use them to help read the text.

- *Repeated sentence or phrase.* The same sentence or phrase is repeated on nearly every page. The repetition helps the young reader use memory to read the sentence or phrase.

- *Rhyme and rhythm.* Both help a child read the text.

- *Cumulative pattern.* As the story progresses, previous lines are repeated, providing the reader with scaffolded practice.

- *Familiar sequence.* Days of the week or counting are two examples of this feature. Students use what they know to help them read the text.

EXAMPLES:
The Deep Blue Sea: A Book of Colors by Audrey Wood
Good Morning, Digger by Anne Rockwell
Mommies Say Shhh! by Patricia Polacco
Why Not? by Mary Wormell
One Red Dot by David A. Carter

WHY USE THEM TO TEACH FLUENCY?
Predictable books are advantageous for several reasons. First, they help children to read with greater ease. Second, reading authentic literature from the very beginning helps children to see that they can read "real" books. Third, although they are most often used with beginning readers, predictable books provide a tremendous amount of support and success for those whose first language is not English and for older children who struggle with reading. Fourth, several predictable books are published in big-book format. They lend themselves to interactive sessions with a large group, helping students to see that they are all a part of the classroom community.

• Information Books (Nonfiction)

DESCRIPTION: Nonfiction books present factual information on a given topic. Most include photographs and illustrations to help students better understand the content.

EXAMPLES:
Baby Sea Otter by Betty Tatham
Into the Ice: The Story of Arctic Exploration by Lynn Curlee
Liberty Rising: The Story of the Statue of Liberty by Pegi Deitz Shea
On Earth by G. Brian Karas

WHY USE THEM TO TEACH FLUENCY?
There are two sound reasons for using information texts. First, they present information about the world around us. Because many children are curious about their surroundings, these texts provide motivating and interesting reading material. Second, the text structures used in information texts differ from those used in fiction. Students need to learn how to read both types of texts to become competent readers.

• Multilevel Books

DESCRIPTION: Multilevel books are written with multiple story lines. Books with simple story lines and more information about specific features in the text at the end of the book are also considered multilevel. While some of these books are fiction, the majority are nonfiction (informational). Still others combine fiction and nonfiction.

EXAMPLES:

A Subway for New York by David Weitzman is a nonfiction selection containing two
    story lines.
Elephants Can Paint, Too by Katya Arnold is another example.
This Rocket by Paul Collicutt is a nonfiction text that has a simple story line with
    accompanying information on the inside front and back covers of the text that
    gives a brief history of rockets (front) and tells about the Apollo 11 Mission (back).
Sharks and Other Dangers of the Deep by Simon Mugford is an example that contains
    three story lines.
Wise Guy: The Life and Philosophy of Socrates by M. D. Usher is an example that con-
    tains two story lines and information at the end of the text.

WHY USE THEM TO TEACH FLUENCY?

The books are rich in content; they contain much information about subjects that
interest children. They also provide for meaningful repeated reading and scaffolding.
That is, once children hear other parts of the story from either the teacher or classmates, they are more likely to be able to read the text themselves. Finally, in terms of
resources, more mileage can be gotten out of fewer dollars.

• Series Books

DESCRIPTION: Series books share elements such as characters, author's style, words,
and format. Children can often follow the development of characters and share in their
adventures in each succeeding book in the series.

EXAMPLES:

Grades 1–2	Gus and Grandpa by Claudia Mills
Grades 2–3	Polk Street Kids by Patricia Reilly Giff
Grades 2–3	Cam Jansen by David A. Adler
Grades 2–5	The Zack Files by Dan Greenburg
Grades 3–4	Hank, the Cowdog by John R. Erickson
Grades 4–6	Harry Potter by J. K. Rowling

WHY USE THEM TO TEACH FLUENCY?

Series books can be very effective because they provide meaningful reading practice.
Once children get hooked on a book in a series, they have a desire to keep reading the
others. Because books in a series share characters, plot structure, and words, the natural
redundancy of these features provides support for the most novice of readers enabling
the child to read the texts. Children gain confidence, not to mention fluency!

• Chapter Books

DESCRIPTION: Chapter books are broken into segments or chapters. They range in difficulty from the first-grade level through the upper elementary grades.

EXAMPLES:

Chapter books for novice readers
Henry and Mudge series by Cynthia Rylant
Frog and Toad series by Arnold Lobel

Chapter books for older readers (the following are recent Newbery Medal and Honor books)
Bud, Not Buddy by Christopher Paul Curtis
Missing May by Cynthia Rylant
The Giver by Lois Lowry
Walk Two Moons by Sharon Creech
Shiloh by Phyllis Naylor

WHY USE THEM TO TEACH FLUENCY?
Chapter books afford children an opportunity to read books that they see in and out of school, in libraries and bookstores. They help students learn how key parts of a story are connected by individual chapters. They also provide logical stopping points to show children how they can use the authors' words to sound just like the character when reading aloud.

• Scripts (Plays and Readers Theater)

DESCRIPTION: Scripts are used in plays and in Readers Theater. The major difference between the two is that plays are usually intended for performance using theatrical features (e.g., props, costumes, stages). Performers have to memorize the script so that they can effectively create the scenes for the audience. Readers Theater, on the other hand, is meant to be performed without props. Students practice reading scripts and, when ready, perform with scripts in hand to an interested audience.

EXAMPLES:

Texts that include scripts

Grades 1–3	*What's the Time, Grandma Wolf?* by Ken Brown
Grades 2–3	*Frog Went A-Courting* by Dominic Catalano
Grades 4–6	*You're On! Seven Plays in English and Spanish* by Lori Carlson
Grades 5–7	*Replay* by Sharon Creech

Don't Speed. READ!

WHY USE THEM TO TEACH FLUENCY?
Plays and Readers Theater can help children develop reading fluency through repeated readings. Repeated readings allow readers to better comprehend the text. Through rereading, students are also able to refine their ideas about the script and the characters it portrays. As a result, they are better able to use speed, accuracy, and prosody to best convey their interpretations of the characters they are playing.

• Magazines

Description: Magazines comprise a multitude of text types and features: articles and stories designed to inform readers of many different topics, columns of text, pictures with captions, short tidbits about different topics, diagrams, and advertisements, to name a few. Most magazines focus on a specific audience and feature articles that would appeal to this audience.

EXAMPLES:
Sesame Street Magazine (ages 0–6)
Zoobooks (ages 6–14)
Cricket Magazine (ages 8–14)

WHY USE THEM TO TEACH FLUENCY?
One of the best reasons for using magazines for teaching fluency is that they are filled with short articles that students can practice with ease, gleaning information they share with interested others. Magazines also seem less intimidating than books to some children, making them feel at ease when reading. Short article reading translates into meaningful reading practice that enhances fluency.

• Newspapers

DESCRIPTION: Newspapers contain information articles, advertisements, photos with captions, comics, and other features designed to inform the public about current events. Most are published daily, although some specifically written for classroom use are published weekly.

EXAMPLES:
Weekly Reader (preschool–grade 6)
Scholastic News (grades 1–6)
Kids page or "Mini Page" from local newspaper (grades 1–3)
Local newspaper (grades 3–6)

WHY USE THEM TO TEACH FLUENCY?

Newspapers provide a wealth of reading material in everyday life. They provide information about current events on several levels. In terms of fluency, newspapers are an excellent resource to teach students about how readers set purposes when reading and how they use speed to accomplish that purpose. Most readers, for example, choose their favorite section of the paper and even then, skim read it, only stopping to read stories that capture their interest. And even then, readers may not read every single word with 100 percent accuracy. They read to get the gist of the article. Because newspapers are written in column format, they offer an authentic way to teach students something about reading in meaningful chunks or phrases. Through newspapers, students better understand how speed, accuracy, and prosody are tools that can assist their reading and comprehension.

• Cyber-Texts

DESCRIPTION: Cyber-texts are texts that exist in electronic digital environments. These texts are primarily accessible through computers and available on the Internet. The increasing proliferation of handheld devices and wireless accessibility means that cyber-texts now can be received and composed virtually anywhere, at any time, by anyone. Kamil, Kim, and Lane (2004) classify electronic text into two primary categories. The first consists of any text found on the computer screen (e-mail messages, help screens, instructions). Such text exists digitally and can be transmitted from one computer to another. Except for navigational differences, readers often approach this text much as they approach print formats. The second category consists of any electronic text augmented by hyperlinks, hypertext, or hypermedia. These texts are more complicated texts and are most often found on the Internet. Augmented texts provide reading experiences that are quite different from those of traditional print formats.

EXAMPLES:

Yahoo! Kids, http://kids.yahoo.com

This is a Web guide for children. As a search engine, it searches for specific information that students request.

Children's Reading Room, http://unmuseum.mus.pa.us/crr/

Here you'll find a selection of stories that children can download and print for their reading. Stories vary in length.

PBS Kids, http://pbskids.org/

Arthur, Barney, and Clifford are but a few of the characters featured on this site. Children can access stories, games, music, and even coloring forms related to different story characters.

Children's Storybooks Online, Stories for Kids of All Ages,
   http://www.magickeys.com/books
   Free storybooks for young and older children and young adults can be found at
   this Web site. Many of the books are illustrated. The site also features riddles,
   puzzles, and information about how to publish a book.
RIF Reading Planet, http://rif.org/readingplanet/
   Reading Is Fundamental's site provides, among other activities, story maker, which
   enables children to personalize stories by adding their own words to them.
   Children can also replace some words in the story and write their own endings.

WHY USE THEM TO TEACH FLUENCY?
Cyber-texts can be highly motivating for students. They see the texts as fun and not
one bit intimidating. As a consequence, they are drawn to these texts and get much
reading practice developing fluency. Some sites have accompanying read-aloud voices;
others provide assistance by highlighting words and speaking the words as students
point the cursor at them. All of this assistance is geared toward helping students read
the text with comprehension and fluency.

• Real-Life Texts

DESCRIPTION: While any text might be considered a real-life text, I see real-life texts as
those written materials that primarily serve a function in nonschool settings. These
materials are not intentionally designed for classroom instructional purposes. I group
real-life texts in the following categories:

- Environmental print (e.g., billboards and advertisements)

- Materials that help us cope with the complexities of life (e.g., directions, manuals,
  menus)

- Materials that may help us deal with time and space (e.g., bus schedules, maps)

- Materials that help us build a sense of community within and across groups (e.g.,
  print at celebrations, sporting events, political rallies)

As you can see from the examples, many of these texts are not in a book format,
and many are readily available for a minimal price or for free.

EXAMPLES:
Environmental Print:
Billboards • Signs • Bumper stickers • Buttons • T-shirts, sweatshirts, hats

Coping With Time:
Bus, train, plane schedules • TV guides • Calendars

Coping With Space:
Maps and directions • Catalogues • Phonebooks • Letters and postcards

Coping With Complexities:
Directions • Manuals • Menus • Applications • Coupons • Advertisements

Building Community:
Logos • Slogans • Banners • Balloons • Cards • Games

WHY USE THEM TO TEACH FLUENCY?
Real-life texts are just that. They exist in our everyday lives. What better way to show students how fluency relates to the real world than to use real-life text? Imagine, for example, how a child might read Nike's "Just Do It!" slogan. Perfect for reading in phrases, don't you think? Or how about the importance of reading with accuracy when reading instructions for video games or following printed directions for assembling a model? Without a doubt, using real-life texts can be an excellent vehicle for teaching students about fluency in meaningful contexts.

• Leveled Books

DESCRIPTION: Leveled books are sets of small books designed for young children. They are usually the same size, with a paperback cover and only a few pages. Often written by different authors, all titles are leveled and then assembled by the publisher to create sets of readers that can be used for small-group reading instruction. Peterson (1991) describes the specific features used to determine a book's level of difficulty (see Figure 6.2).

EXAMPLES:
Sets of little books, available from a number of publishers, include the following:
Literacy by Design (Harcourt-Achieve)
Windows on Literacy (National Geographic)
People, Spaces & Places (Rand McNally)

WHY USE THEM TO TEACH FLUENCY?
Little books are especially designed for use with beginning readers, sometimes starting in kindergarten and continuing through the elementary school grades. The texts become increasingly difficult as the grades progress. The leveled texts are usually packaged in multiple sets, six copies per set. One way the books can be used is in small-

FIGURE 6.2

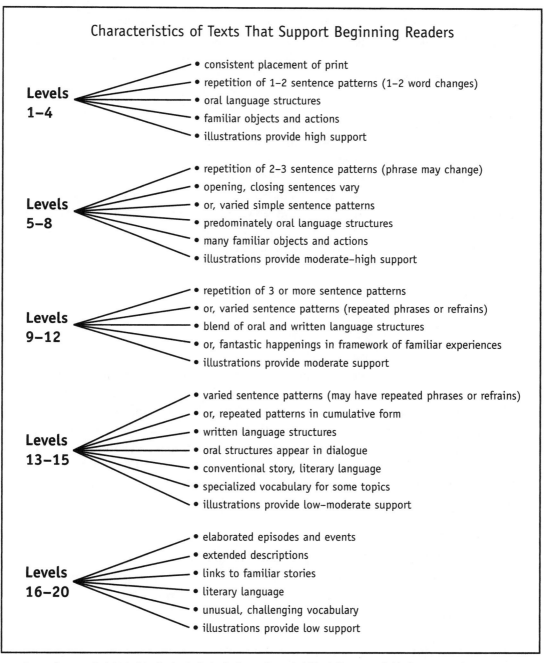

Characteristics of Texts That Support Beginning Readers

Levels 1–4
- consistent placement of print
- repetition of 1–2 sentence patterns (1–2 word changes)
- oral language structures
- familiar objects and actions
- illustrations provide high support

Levels 5–8
- repetition of 2–3 sentence patterns (phrase may change)
- opening, closing sentences vary
- or, varied simple sentence patterns
- predominately oral language structures
- many familiar objects and actions
- illustrations provide moderate–high support

Levels 9–12
- repetition of 3 or more sentence patterns
- or, varied sentence patterns (repeated phrases or refrains)
- blend of oral and written language structures
- or, fantastic happenings in framework of familiar experiences
- illustrations provide moderate support

Levels 13–15
- varied sentence patterns (may have repeated phrases or refrains)
- or, repeated patterns in cumulative form
- written language structures
- oral structures appear in dialogue
- conventional story, literary language
- specialized vocabulary for some topics
- illustrations provide low–moderate support

Levels 16–20
- elaborated episodes and events
- extended descriptions
- links to familiar stories
- literary language
- unusual, challenging vocabulary
- illustrations provide low support

Source: Peterson, B. (1991). Selecting books for beginning readers and children's literature suitable for young readers. In D. DeFord, C. Lyons & G. Pinnell (Eds.), *Bridges to literacy: Learning from reading recovery* (pp. 119–147). Portsmouth, NH: Heinemann.

group settings. The teacher first models fluent reading, in whole or in part, depending on the focus of the lesson. After modeling, students can then read their own copies. Because the books have so few pages, students can read through the books many times within a matter of minutes. This rereading is one way to improve all aspects of fluency (Allington, 2006; Clay, 1991).

• Basal Readers

DESCRIPTION: Basal readers are the central components of commercially developed reading programs. They are often structured as anthologies of grade-leveled texts packaged with a number of support materials such as teacher guides and student workbooks. They are most often selected and purchased to provide a cohesive, consistent, continuous reading curriculum across and between grade levels throughout a school district or an individual school. In most classrooms, each child is provided a copy of the anthology (e.g., reader) to use during guided reading.

EXAMPLES:
Treasures (McGraw-Hill, 2005)
Houghton Mifflin Reading (2003)
Reading Street (Scott Foresman, 2006)

WHY USE THEM TO TEACH FLUENCY?
The better question might be, "Why not?" They are available to teachers and students as the result of district-wide adoptions and most teachers are expected to use them. The selections are, to some extent, organized by the level of sophistication of their vocabulary, concepts, and text structures so that they can be used to scaffold instruction. In fact, two researchers have discovered that using a grade-level anthology, though at the frustration level for some, can indeed improve children's reading ability, particularly fluency, if students are given adequate support and several opportunities to practice some or all of a given selection (Kuhn & Stahl, 2000).

• Textbooks

DESCRIPTION: Besides the materials purchased for and used in the classroom reading/language arts program, a number of other commercially prepared texts are designed for instruction in specific content areas such as science, social studies, and mathematics. Often, one series is selected for a school district or school. A series most often comprises a set of common core texts, each containing appropriate grade-level presentations of increasingly sophisticated subject-area content. Each student is provided a copy of the grade-level text.

EXAMPLES:

Super Study Skills by Laurie Rozakis (Scholastic)

Science Explorer (Prentice-Hall)

Social Studies: Regions and Resources (Silver Burdett Ginn)

WHY USE THEM TO TEACH FLUENCY?

One of the most important ideas we want to convey to students is that fluency can help them in all content areas. If students understand how to adjust reading rate to purpose, for example, they can think about what they know about the text they will be reading and what they are trying to achieve in reading it. They can then proceed to read at a pace that will enable them to comprehend the text, regardless of content area. Likewise, if students understand how authors use signals such as punctuation markings and italic and bold print to best convey their ideas, students can use this knowledge to comprehend the text at hand. Without a doubt, we want students to understand that fluency serves a purpose and that it isn't something that happens at a given time of day. The goal is to improve students' ability to use fluency as they negotiate their way through different content-area texts with maximum comprehension.

There are many different kinds of texts that we can use to teach children about fluency in meaningful contexts. All of them have the potential to show children how fluency relates to real reading, both in and out of school.

➔ REFLECTION ⇒

Having read about these many different kinds of texts, which might you use to teach fluency? How would you use them? Take some time to reflect and write your responses in the chart on the next page.

TEXTS FOR TEACHING FLUENCY

Text Type	How and When You Might Use It
Song texts	
Poetry	
Predictable books	
Information (nonfiction)	
Multilevel literature	
Series books	
Chapter books	
Scripts	
Magazines	
Newspapers	
Cyber-texts	
Real-life texts	
Leveled books	
Basal readers	
Textbooks	

Don't Speed. READ!

Establish a Nurturing Environment

Safe, *risk-free*, and *comfortable* are three terms that come to mind when I think about having students further their understanding of reading fluency. As teachers we need to create a nurturing environment so that students can feel at ease when communicating with one another. Without this type of environment, many of the fluency activities in Step 5 are doomed to failure because each calls on students to communicate with others in a group. Imagine how difficult it would be to share a poem with an entire class or even a group if you did not feel that you were in a safe, risk-free, and comfortable environment! It would put a damper on your ability to use speed, accuracy, and prosody to communicate your understanding of the poem with others. In this instance, you would use speed, accuracy, and prosody as survival techniques to achieve your primary goal of not embarrassing yourself. Communicating ideas would be the last thing on your mind.

Creating a nurturing environment is a personal matter because we all have our unique ways of showing students that we are interested in their well-being. Some teachers show children how to nurture one another by caring for classroom pets. My son's second-grade teacher used plants. Student desks were arranged in pods of four and each pod took care of a plant. The same teacher used music, selecting songs for children to learn that emphasized caring for one another. Regardless of your personal style, here are seven ideas that are surefire ways to create a nurturing environment.

Ensure that all learners feel that they're part of the community.

For *community*, we might apply this practical definition: "A place in which students feel cared about and are encouraged to care about each other. They experience a sense of being valued and respected; the children matter to one another and to the teacher. They have come to think in the plural; they feel connected to each other; they are part of an 'us'" (Kohn, 1996, p. 101).

> "When we are valued for the human beings we are, we become less threatened by others, we feel safe, then we feel successful and accepted."
>
> *Nina Zargoza*

As this definition relates to fluency instruction, then, providing children with opportunities to work with many different classmates is a way to help them feel part of the classroom community. For example, Partner Reading (see page 118) calls on students to work with a partner to share information and use fluency in a meaningful context. Readers Theater (see page 119) offers opportunities for students to work with larger groups to prepare a reading of a play for an interested audience. As a result of interacting with one another, students are more likely to feel connected; they see how they are contributing to shared knowledge. As a result of listening to one another, students are more likely to see additional ways to interpret text and gain new insights. And in both of these activities, the overriding concern is communicating information with others and developing fluency along the way. That is, students learn that the aspects of fluency—appropriate speed, accuracy, and prosody—help them convey the author's intended meaning to their listeners.

Use small groups to help children better understand what they have read.

Smaller groups of varying sizes increase student participation. They afford more opportunities for students to paraphrase, explain, and elaborate on a given text. What better way for students to understand how the different components of fluency are used in oral language as well as written? Take speed, for example. As they are sharing, students have to alter their speed so that their audience will stay with them and understand what they are saying.

Enable students to work cooperatively with a wide variety of peers.

Working in many different types of groupings gives students an opportunity to work with all classmates. Because the emphasis is on enhancing students' oral fluency to communicate, rather than to target reading level, students of varying levels can be placed together. When preparing a Readers Theater script, for instance, students can be assigned parts according to their ability to read given parts.

Help students feel more involved with their learning.

Interest is a major contributing factor in learning to read. One of the best ways to engage students and encourage them to use fluency for communicating ideas is to allow them to form groups based on their interests. Students who are interested in animals, for example, could silently read materials on the topic and prepare to share some facts with interested partners or a group. In preparing for the sharing, students are able to practice using appropriate speed, accuracy, and prosody so that they can later share aloud with ease and confidence.

Use flexible grouping as a way to engage students with appropriate instruction and materials.

When we think about how much more time we have to talk when we are with a small group, it should come as no surprise that using flexible grouping enhances fluency. When students engage in a discussion over what has been shared by another in the group, not only do they have greater gains in reading achievement (Almasi, McKeown, & Beck, 1996; Manning & Manning, 1984), they also further their understanding of how fluency relates to oral language.

Steer clear of ability grouping.

There is a wealth of research findings on the devastating effects of ability grouping (see Opitz, 1998, for a review of research), often defined as "the placement of students according to similar levels of intelligence or achievement in some skill or subject, either within or among classes or schools" (Harris & Hodges, 1995, p. 2).

Although these findings are research-based—and being research-based is of utmost importance in the new millennium—they appear to be ignored. Ability grouping is heavily used in the name of "good" fluency instruction. But there is little good about it. Take, for example, the school staff that is coerced into giving timed, cold-read "fluency tests" to determine the words per minute that children read. As if the test alone isn't bad enough, the children are then grouped for reading instruction by their overall scores. Fifth-grade children who score 124 words per minute are placed in a "bench-mark" group whereas those who score 123 and below are placed in the "intensive" group. Each group then receives different reading instruction because that is what their speed score indicates they need. What are children to think of themselves and reading when they are grouped in this manner? Is it any wonder that so many of them think of themselves as incompetent readers, when they are told that speed is the only measure of reader competence and the main purpose for reading?

Now let's think about it in terms of what children perceive about reading fluency. Not surprisingly, when they hear fluency and speed used synonymously, speed takes center stage to the exclusion of accuracy, let alone prosody, when reading aloud.

Let me be perfectly clear: When we group children in this manner and misuse terms, we actually thwart their progress rather than advance it. Many times, children's misunderstandings about reading in general and fluency in particular show themselves as reading problems and take much time to remediate. What is most troubling to me is that students' misunderstandings are too quickly dismissed as student-centered learn-ing problems when in fact they are not. More often than not, they are the result of poor instruction to which the student attended all too well.

Listen to students.

When we pay attention to students both verbally and nonverbally, we show them that what they have to offer matters. Modeling attentive listening is a good first step toward showing, rather than telling, students to listen to one another. This being said, in order for us to model active listening, we need to believe the following:

- Teacher talk is not always necessary for teaching and learning.

- Learning how to think is most important.

- Questions we ask need to encourage thinking.

- Children are capable of constructing good questions.

- All need to listen to one another.

- Listening and talking are ways to resolve issues.

How important listening is to the development of fluency! Said another way, when reading aloud, why would one go through the effort of trying to use appropriate speed, accuracy, and prosody without an interested audience?

→ REFLECTION →

And so I return to the terms *safe*, *risk-free*, and *comfortable* to describe a nurturing environment conducive to facilitating language growth in general and fluency in particular. Take some time to think about the words you would add to the list and jot them in the space below.

NURTURING ENVIRONMENT WORDS

_____

_____

_____

_____

_____

_____

_____

Plan Effective Instruction

A glance into Susan's second-grade classroom reveals children reading a variety of texts to themselves. Some sit at desks, and others are nestled under them, creating a cozy reading nook. Still others are sprinkled throughout the room, some lying on the floor or sitting in the rocking chair.

Josh has just finished assessing some third-grade students using a text that students have had ample time to practice. The purpose of his assessment was to discover how students use speed, accuracy, and prosody when reading. He will use the results to plan instruction to heighten students' awareness of different aspects of fluency as needed.

How are both of these teachers enabling children to develop reading fluency? Before reading further, think about this question and discuss it with a colleague.

I suspect that in your discussion, several ideas emerged about how each teacher is enabling children to become more fluent readers. The main point I want to emphasize is that while both teachers are facilitating fluency development, the first is using informal instruction while the second is using formal instruction. It is explicit instruction, designed with specific objectives and students in mind. It is driven by ongoing (i.e., formative) assessment. And it is what this step is all about.

You might be wondering why I would choose to emphasize explicit instruction over more informal instruction, so let me explain. If your interactions with children have been anything like mine, you know that there are those students who seem to need little if any instruction. They seem to have caught the reading habit and adopted the behaviors of proficient readers naturally. Nonetheless, these children continue to refine their understandings about reading by exploring how to best communicate information to others and how to improve their comprehension. Because these children already have an understanding of how reading operates, they are in a better position to understand how the components of fluency affect readers and listeners alike, through informal instruction.

But what about the many children who have not acquired proficient reading behaviors? How can we best help them? In addition to informal instruction, these children need more explicit instruction. The purpose of this step, then, is to provide you with some suggestions on how to plan for this type of instruction.

Before delving into the intricacies of planning instruction I want to clarify what I mean by "proficient reading behaviors." We need to know exactly what these behaviors are before we can start planning fluency instruction to help children acquire proficient reading behaviors. Figure 8.1 summarizes Steven Kucer's research (2005) classifying proficient and less proficient reading behaviors.

FIGURE 8.1

Summary of Proficient and Less Proficient Reading Behaviors

Proficient Reading Behaviors	*Less Proficient Reading Behaviors*
1. Attempt to make what is read sound like language and make sense	Attempt to identify all of the words correctly
2. Monitor what is read for sense and coherence	Monitor what is read for correct letter/sound and word identification
3. Build meaning using the text, their purpose, and their background	Build meaning by attempting to identify the letters and words correctly
4. Utilize a variety of strategies when meaning breaks down: reread, rethink, read on and return if necessary, substitute, skip it, sound out, seek assistance, use text aids (pictures, graphs, charts), ignore it, stop reading	Utilize a limited range of strategies when meaning breaks down: sound out, skip it
5. Selectively sample the print; use a mixture of visual (print) and nonvisual (background) information	Utilize most of the visual (print) information
6. Use and integrate a variety of systems of language to create meaning	Rely heavily on graphemes, graphophonemics, and morphemes
7. Vary the manner in which texts are read based on purpose	Read all texts in a similar manner regardless of purpose
8. Typically correct one in three miscues	Typically correct one in twenty miscues
9. Attempt to correct miscues that affect meaning	Attempt to correct miscues that fail to resemble the word
10. "Chunk" what is read	Process letter-by-letter, which results in tunnel vision

Source: Adapted from Kucer, S. (2005). *The dimensions of literacy: A conceptual base for teaching reading and writing in school settings* (2nd ed.). Mahwah, NJ: Erlbaum.

We can see that proficient readers have a large repertoire of strategies at their disposal to help themselves better comprehend the text at hand. The strategies they employ will shift according to their background for the text and the manner in which the text is written.

Several of the proficient reading behaviors Kucer lists specifically relate to fluency. For example, the first calls attention to making what is read sound like language. This is the essence of prosody. The seventh attribute calls attention to speed, and the eighth and ninth point to accuracy. The ability to chunk, the last attribute, is nothing more than prosody, more specifically phrasing.

Finally, we can see those who carry the "proficient reader" label are most often fluent readers, yet there are children who carry the "fluent reader" label who, according to these criteria, are not proficient. These are readers who sound fluent in terms of prosody yet show little understanding of what they have read. Likewise, they may read at breakneck speed and read with accuracy, demonstrating that they don't understand that they need to vary how a text is read depending on their purpose (one attribute of a proficient reader) or that miscues can be acceptable (another attribute of a proficient reader). What we want, then, are *proficient readers who are fluent* rather than *fluent readers who are not proficient.*

So how should we design instruction to create proficient readers who are fluent? The previous steps in this book help to answer this question. You have a wealth of information to guide your planning as a result of:

- thinking through your fluency definition and your view of teaching reading— and aligning these with your fluency assessment
- understanding how to use students as informants
- exploring a variety of fluency activities and types of texts
- learning ways to cultivate a nurturing environment

You also have your own teaching experiences to add to the mix.

In *Flexible Grouping in Reading* (1998), I offer suggestions for planning reading instruction so that all children can succeed. With some modifications, these suggestions ring true for fluency instruction as well. In fact, flexible grouping and fluency instruction are a good fit. For instance, one guiding principle of flexible grouping and fluency instruction alike is that assessment guides instruction. We use the results to determine how to best use the available time to help all students. Whole-group and small-group instruction are both viable alternatives (see Step 5 for additional information about grouping structures). Any time we group students, we have to consider the purpose for establishing the group and once the purpose has been achieved, the group dissolves.

Flexible grouping is also a key component of fluency activities. As noted in Step 5, different fluency activities call for different grouping structures. Often more than one structure is used within a given activity.

Without further ado, then, here are some planning suggestions:

Use a three-phase instructional framework to ensure the success of all students.

The one shown in Figure 8.2 was originally developed by Herber in 1978 as a way for teachers of content areas to better plan their instruction. Since that time, the three-part

FIGURE 8.2

Three-Phase Framework

Instructional Phase	Purpose
Before Reading	Prepare students for reading: • Activate or build background knowledge. • Arouse curiosity. • Address any individual needs. • Set the purpose.
During Reading	Provide time for students to read.
After Reading	Provide an opportunity for students to demonstrate understanding of the reading and attain the purpose of the lesson.

structure has become commonplace in most elementary classrooms. As Reutzel's daily lesson framework (2006) demonstrates, this structure enables the teacher to support learners at every phase and gradually release the learning onto the students' shoulders.

Decide on the purpose for the lesson.

According to your analysis of assessment results, what is it that students need to learn about fluency? Which students appear to need further help with this aspect of fluency?

To better help children understand that fluency fits into a larger reading scheme, you might want to integrate the fluency instruction with a specific content area. And to keep students focused on comprehension, you might also want to focus on reading comprehension. In Step 9, I provide some explanation and ideas for how to best accomplish this integration.

Select the texts that will best help you to accomplish your purpose.

As discussed in Step 6, there are many different kinds of texts that you can use to teach students about fluency. Each text type is appropriate for particular purposes. For example, if students need to learn something about prosody, and phrasing in particular, you might want to use poetry or predictable books.

Think about how you need to group students to best accomplish your purpose.

As mentioned in Step 5, there are different ways to group students, and each has its advantages and disadvantages. If all students in your class need to learn a particular fluency skill, you may want to use the whole-class grouping structure to best utilize your time. At other times, you might decide to use different grouping structures within different phases of your lesson to best help you achieve your purpose. For instance, you might start with the whole class for the prereading activity, move to small groups during reading itself, and return to the large group after reading.

Select appropriate teaching strategies.

As I show in Step 5, we are not at a loss for fluency teaching strategies. In fact, the abundance can be overwhelming. Perhaps the best way to select a strategy is to think about what it is that you are trying to accomplish. Say, for example, you want students to learn how to read a grade-level textbook with fluency and understanding. You know that the text will be difficult for some students and just right for others. You decide to use the Fluency Oriented Reading Lesson (see pages 117–118) because it will provide students with much support at the start of the lesson and with needed meaningful practice throughout the week.

Another way to choose a strategy is to consider the type of text that you want to use to help you accomplish your purpose. As Figure 6.1 (page 43) shows, some texts lend themselves to specific fluency activities.

Gather all necessary materials.

Explicit teaching requires preparation. Making sure that all materials are at hand leads to greater success.

Concerned about remembering all of these considerations? Use the lesson plan form shown in Step 9 (page 74) to help you to plan for success—yours and the students' alike. There is space provided for you to add your content area, comprehension objective, and fluency objective. On the left side it lists the considerations that you need to think through. The right side provides some space for you to write notes to yourself for each lesson phase.

REFLECTION

Use the following prompts to further think about what you have read and as starting points for a discussion with your colleagues.

• Think about how what you have read here might connect with what you already do in terms of planning for explicit instruction.

• Think about your definition of fluency, view of reading, assessment, and instruction. How do they align?

• How can you make sure that you plan fluency instruction that will enable children to acquire proficient reading behaviors, rather than less proficient reading behaviors?

Notes

Don't Speed. READ!

Show Children How Fluency Fits Into the Larger Reading Scheme

"I read the word problem but I still don't know if I am supposed to add or subtract," John, a second-grade student in Bill's class, comments.

"Read it to me," Bill responds. As John reads, Bill notes that John reads the problem so quickly that he pays little attention to understanding the words that signal which mathematical operation to use. In fact, he miscues on a key word, saying "today" for the printed word *together*. Once John has finished reading, Bill comments, "I think I see why you might not know what you are supposed to do to solve this problem, John. Try reading it to me again, but this time, I want you to read it like you are talking to me to help me understand the problem. Please read it more slowly so that I can better understand." John rereads the text following Bill's advice. Before he is finished, he begins to smile.

"Why the smile, John?"

"I know I am supposed to add because I see the words *and* and *all together*," John responds.

"So you figured out the problem by slowing down and paying attention to understanding what you are reading. It's not enough to read quickly, is it? What's most important is understanding what you read. This means that sometimes you need to read more slowly. And especially when reading word problems, you need to read every word just as it is printed."

John returns to his desk to complete the computation and to read and solve other word problems. Bill is pleased that John is aware of speed when reading because this is one aspect of fluency that he has been teaching his students. He is also pleased to see that John was able to detect where his understanding breaks down and that he used appropriate fix-up strategies to take care of the problem. Both show that John has developed a self-extending system (Clay, 1983), one important attribute of proficient reading.

But the reading problem is anything but resolved for Bill. Bill also sees that he needs to help students like John to further understand how readers need to adjust the speed of reading with their purpose for reading, and that doing so is one hallmark of a proficient reader (Kucer, 2005). He recognizes that in his future instruction, he needs to show students how to best use elements of fluency, not to mention comprehension, across all content areas including mathematics. Bill feels certain that through such instruction his students will see that fluency, or any other reading skill for that matter, is anything but a one-time event that happens during the scheduled reading time. Instead, the skills are complementary and lasting and they assist readers in their journey to understanding a variety of texts.

So often, though, it seems as if we look for the single silver bullet that will solve all reading problems. A few years ago, phonological awareness was catapulted into the media spotlight by claims that it is the best predictor of reading success. As a result, children were (and still are) provided numerous phonological lessons, needed or not. Yet reading problems persist. Now many see reading fluency as the answer to reading problems. No longer neglected (Allington, 1983), it is now front and center in reading programs and reading instruction. Are reading problems likely to disappear as a result? Not likely. Reading is complex, and many factors contribute to successful reading comprehension.

As Bill shows, this silver-bullet mind-set need not be the only approach. One of the ways we can guard against simplifying reading, both for ourselves and for students like John, is to *show* them as much as *tell* them how we use reading skills when reading all types of texts in many different content areas. Bill also helps us to see the time we can save by integrating fluency instruction into already existing classroom structures. Rather than wonder how we are going to carve out some time for teaching fluency, we can use the framework we already have in place.

Consider Rachel, a fifth-grade teacher who wants her students to learn more about natural disasters during social studies. Taking a look at the text, she knows that it is at the students' instructional level and that they will be able to read it without much difficulty. She also knows that she can help students make connections to natural disasters by reading them a current newspaper article about Hurricane Katrina. She has two purposes in mind for this lesson. First, she wants students to comprehend the selection. In particular, she wants to provide students with practice using the "determining importance" strategy. Second, she wants her students to learn more about reading fluency. She wants students to understand the importance of phrasing, intonation and expression (prosody) when reading to others.

Using the three-phase lesson plan described in Step 8, Rachel opens the lesson by reading the newspaper article to her students (see Figure 9.1). Once finished, she thinks aloud to model determining importance: "The author of this article has included a lot of information. But I think what is most important are her points about the hardship that the hurricane is causing many different people." On a transparency that displays the article, she underlines the points she thinks are most important as students watch.

She then reads one of the points aloud to students and reminds students of how important it is to read with expression and phrasing so that the reading sounds more like talking. She comments, "Reading aloud this way helps the listener better understand what you are trying to communicate." Finally, she tells students why she identified this one point to read aloud.

Rachel then tells students that hurricanes are only one type of natural disaster. She asks for volunteers to name other kinds of natural disasters and writes their ideas on the board using a semantic map. Next, she tells students that they will be reading about different kinds of natural disasters in their social studies book over the next few days, starting today with earthquakes. She directs them to the pages in the text and explains the procedures for reading the text: "Today you are going to be reading to yourself and to a partner. You have been learning about how to determine importance when reading to best comprehend, and today you are going to get some practice." She continues: "You have also been learning about the importance of fluency when reading. In particular, what you are going to practice today is phrasing, intonation, and expression. All three are important when reading to others so that you can convey the author's intended meaning. You are going to read your text the same way I read the article. Here's what you do." Rachel displays a transparency with directions on the overhead projector.

TRANSPARENCY: Determining Importance/Fluency

1. Silently read the section entitled "Earthquakes."

2. Using the highlighter tape, highlight at least three ideas that you think are important.

3. Practice reading one of the three ideas to yourself. Practice it at least three times so that when you are reading it to another person, you sound like you are talking.

4. Think about why the idea is important to you and be ready to state your reason to your partner.

5. If you finish reading your article before I tell you that it is time to read to your partner, read another text, such as the one you are reading during independent silent reading.

Students then silently read the article, making their notations. Rachel circulates, providing guidance as needed. Once she sees that everyone has finished the reading, she calls the students back together. "It looks to me as if you have all had time to read, identify what you think is important, and to practice reading one of your ideas. Now it's time to pair up. With your partner, please do the following." She displays a second transparency on the overhead projector, showing the next steps.

FIGURE 9.1

Rachel's Integrated Fluency Lesson

Content Area: Social studies
Comprehension Objective: To provide students with practice using determining importance
Fluency Objective: To provide practice using phrasing, intonation, and expression
Text(s): Newspaper article; p. 185 of social studies text

Considerations	*Teaching Notes*
Before Reading Grouping Technique (check all that apply): **X** whole group ___ small groups of _____ ___ individual *Fluency Teaching Strategy:* • Read-aloud *Other Teaching Strategy:* • Think-aloud, Brainstorming *Materials:* newspaper article, pen, markers	1. Tell students that you read an article in last night's paper that you want to share with them. 2. Read aloud the newspaper article. 3. Model determining importance using think-aloud. 4. Underline three key points in articles as students watch. 5. Practice reading one point, then read it to the students, noting how you read it as if you were talking. 6. Brainstorm natural disasters and make a semantic map with natural disasters as the defined center and their ideas stemming from it.
During Reading Grouping Technique (check all that apply): **X** whole group ___ small groups of _____ **X** individual *Fluency Teaching Strategy:* • Repeated reading *Materials:* Social studies text, highlighter tape, overhead transparency #1	1. Explain the reading procedure to students saying something like, "You are going to read your book the same way I read the newspaper article. But instead of reading your idea to the class, you will be reading aloud to a partner." 2. Display directions using transparency #1. 3. Refer students to social studies text. 4. Provide time for students to read while you circulate and provide assistance as needed.
After Reading Grouping Technique (check all that apply): **X** whole group **X** small groups of __*2*__ ___ individual *Fluency Teaching Strategy:* •Partner reading *Materials:* Social studies text, notebook paper, pencils	1. Explain procedure for partner reading using transparency #2. 2. Provide time for volunteers to share information with the class. 3. Close the lesson saying something like: "You accomplished a lot today! Let's think about what you did." Elicit comments from students. Add comments as needed so that students see that they practiced using determining importance and fluency in addition to learning more about natural disasters. 4. Collect students' written responses.

TRANSPARENCY: Determining Importance/Fluency

1. In turn, take on the role of reader and listener.
    • READER ROLE: Read your statement orally and state why you think it is important. Remember that you want to read like you are talking to one another.
    • LISTENER ROLE: Look at the reader and listen to what is being said. Once the reader is finished, you can give feedback on both the stated idea, the reason for selecting it, and the oral reading. Did it sound like talk? Was it easy to understand?

2. On another sheet of paper, please write how you determined that your stated idea was important and why it is important to you.

The procedures in place, students pair up and share information. When they're finished, Rachel collects the articles and written statements as evidence that students read the article and to assess the degree to which students were able to determine importance. She also closes the lesson by having students reflect on what they accomplished.

In this lesson, fluency is embedded into a larger scheme that establishes an authentic reason for using fluency. Because this is a review lesson, however, it does not show how students are initially taught to determine importance or to read using phrasing, intonation, and expression.

Enter Dan, a third-grade teacher whose observations have helped him to see that his students enjoy reading magazines. He decides to use their interest in magazines to his best advantage. He will use magazines to teach students how to skim to locate specific information and how to adjust reading speed for the purpose of skimming. He will also integrate this lesson with his animal unit in science by having students read *Zoobooks* magazine.

Like Rachel, he uses the three-part lesson plan because he understands the importance of both teacher explanation and modeling as well as the importance of guiding students during and after reading. As Figure 9.2 shows, he begins the lesson with the whole class by telling them he's noticed that they read magazines during their independent reading time. He continues by asking questions. "So when you read your magazines, what do you do? Do you read every article? Do you look at the advertisements? Do you read picture captions? Do you read it in order or do you skip around?" Students are quick to provide insights.

After listening to several volunteer responses, Dan capitalizes on their comments: "So magazines can be read in many different ways. Today I want to focus on something you seem to sometimes do without realizing it. When you glance at pictures or look through your magazine to find specific information, you are *skimming*. Skimming is very helpful for readers because it saves much time and helps them identify what they want to know. This is a skill we use when reading magazines, but it is also useful for any kind of text when we are looking for specific information. Any time you skim-read, you read quickly because you are looking for specific information. You don't need to read all of the words. Quick reading and skimming are a good fit. We're going to practice skimming during small-group guided reading using these magazines." He holds up several copies of *Zoobooks* magazines. Each issue focuses on a different animal.

The lesson continues with Dan teaching students in groups of five. A pile of six *Zoobooks* magazines is in the center of the table. After students are settled, Dan provides them with directions on an overhead transparency. He reads each direction aloud and models it.

TRANSPARENCY: Skimming

1. Select one magazine from the center of the table. To save time, simply take the magazine that is on the top of the pile.

2. Within two minutes, skim through your magazine and locate one fact about your particular animal.

3. Remember that you read quickly when skimming because you do not need to read every word. You are looking for specific information.

4. When I call time, please stop your reading.

5. Share the fact you learned about your animal.

6. Pass your magazine to the person on your right and repeat steps 2–5.

He gives students time to select their magazines and to complete the skimming. Once the two minutes have lapsed he calls "Stop" and gives each student time to share what they discovered. Then students rotate their magazines to the left and repeat the process. He provides assistance as needed. Once all groups have met with him, Dan gathers the whole class together to conclude the lesson.

A close look at this lesson shows that Dan is teaching students about skimming a science text and adjusting reading speed to the purpose. Although he does not explicitly teach it, students are also learning how to share information with others and how to listen to what others have to say. As with Rachel's lesson, Dan's lesson shows his students how fluency fits into the larger reading scheme.

Yet another way that both Rachel and Dan can continue to show their students how fluency fits into the larger reading scheme is by having students use different types of text over the course of the year. Students can experience firsthand that fluency and

FIGURE 9.2

Dan's Integrated Fluency Lesson

Content Area: Science
Comprehension Objective: To provide students with an understanding of skimming to locate specific information
Fluency Objective: To provide students with an understanding of how to adjust reading rate to the purpose for reading
Text(s): *Zoobooks* magazines

Considerations	*Teaching Notes*
Before Reading Grouping Technique (check all that apply): **X** whole group ___ small groups of _____ ___ individual *Other Teaching Strategy:* • Whole-group discussion	1. Discuss with students how they read magazines. 2. Point out that magazines can be read in different ways. 3. Tell students that you are going to show them how to skim to find key information in a magazine and why it's important to know how to skim. 4. Explain how quick reading and skimming go together.
During Reading Grouping Technique (check all that apply): ___ whole group **X** small groups of **5** ___ individual *Fluency Teaching Strategy:* • Read around *Materials:* *Zoobooks* magazines	1. Display transparency #1. 2. As you state each direction, model it so that students will see what they need to do. 3. Provide students with time to read and share information.
After Reading Grouping Technique (check all that apply): **X** whole group ___ small groups of _____ ___ individual *Other Teaching Strategy:* • Whole-group discussion	1. Once all groups have met with you, reconvene the whole class and ask for volunteers to share new information they've learned about any animal. 2. Elicit comments from students about their work skimming. Add comments as needed so that students see that they learned how to skim to locate specific information and how to adjust their speed of reading with their purpose for reading. You might also want to say: "Skimming is an important way of reading when you are trying to locate a specific idea or information. This kind of reading calls for you to read quickly because you do not need to read all words. Knowing your purpose for reading helps you know how to set the correct pace to read the text."

FIGURE 9.3

Integrated Fluency Lesson Plan Form

Content area _____

Comprehension Objective _____

Fluency Objective_____

Text(s) _____

Considerations	*Teaching Notes*
Before Reading Grouping Technique (check all that apply): __ whole group __ small groups of _____ __ individual *Fluency Teaching Strategy:* *Other Teaching Strategies:* *Materials:*	
During Reading Grouping Technique (check all that apply): __ whole group __ small groups of _____ __ individual *Fluency Teaching Strategy:* *Other Teaching Strategies:* *Materials:*	
After Reading Grouping Technique (check all that apply): __ whole group __ small groups of _____ __ individual *Fluency Teaching Strategy:* *Other Teaching Strategies:* *Materials:*	

Don't Speed. READ!

other reading skills are used with all types of texts; they are not reserved for one type of text. Without a doubt, Rachel's and Dan's lessons exemplify showing students how fluency fits into the larger reading scheme. They also exemplify planning for student success by thinking through the lesson considerations in Step 8.

The lesson plan form shown in Figure 9.3 can serve as a reminder of elements to consider as you plan an integrated fluency lesson. Use it as is or adapt it to fit your needs.

→ REFLECTION →

These are just a few ways to show students how fluency fits into the larger reading scheme. You are sure to think of other ways to integrate fluency into the content areas as well as into your current reading framework, which is the purpose of this reflection. Here are some questions to guide your reflection and discussion with colleagues: How would you integrate fluency with the read-aloud part of your overall reading framework? How might you integrate it with shared reading, guided reading, and independent silent reading?

FLUENCY IN THE LARGER READING SCHEME

Reading Framework	Teaching Ideas
Read-Aloud	
Shared Reading	
Guided Reading	
Independent Reading	
Specific Content Area	

Provide Plenty of Time for Independent Silent Reading

The pianist walks on stage followed by the page-turner. After taking the necessary bows, they seat themselves and the music begins. As a result of following the music and paying attention to the slightest nod from the pianist, the page-turner knows that it is time to turn the page, even though there are two measures on the page that remain to be played. The pianist's eyes have moved well ahead of the musical score and recorded the measures to memory so that they can be played while the page is being turned. Doing so is an essential skill. It enables the music to flow without hesitation. How did the pianist learn this most important skill? Through meaningful practice well ahead of the performance before an audience.

The same can be said for reading fluency. Providing time for students to read silently helps them develop the ability to have their eyes move ahead of the text. This enables them to read without hesitation. In Betts's words, "The individual develops a desirable eye-voice span" (1946, p. 385). Silent reading also fosters increased vocabulary growth (Anderson, 1996) and comprehension (Guthrie, Wigfield, Metsala, & Cox, 1999; Linehart, Zigmond, & Cooley, 1981; Reutzel & Hollingsworth, 1991).

There is ample evidence to support what seems like common sense: students who read more are better readers (see Allington, 2006 for a review of several research findings as well as Krashen, 2004). As with any other activity that we want to perfect, meaningful practice in reading matters. Given that a key purpose of silent reading is to understand the material, it seems that it is a necessary first step if we want students to express this meaning to others through oral reading. To underscore the importance of silent reading as an aid to fluency development, I've included it in nearly every fluency activity described in this book.

Despite the importance of independent silent reading (i.e., scheduled time when students select their own texts and independently read them without interruption) some teachers are reluctant to have students engage in it. One concern is that they will be unable to check on students' reading in general and their reading fluency in particular. I imagine that this concern is fueled by the current emphasis on accountability. We as teachers feel we must show evidence of growth for nearly every activity students perform. Although I can understand this feeling, I think we also need to remember that independent silent reading is a time for students to practice without penalty. The evidence of their growth comes later, when we provide some sort of assessment. I liken this to the time I spent in the practice room following my weekly voice lesson. The voice teacher certainly could not be present for every practice session to determine if I was really practicing and if I was practicing the assigned material. The proof of my practice (or lack thereof) would come the following voice lesson, when I had to perform the assigned selections. My voice teacher had to trust me just as we must trust our students.

I know: While you might agree with my thoughts, you might be in a situation that calls on you to document that learning occurred even during independent silent reading time. This need not be a problem. For example, once silent reading time is finished, students can engage in conversation with others about what they read and make comments in a reading journal. Using a form similar to the Independent Silent Reading Log (Appendix A, page 112), they can also record what they read, including the date, title, and a brief evaluation of the text or something they learned by reading it. Finally, you can observe what they were reading and make notes for yourself using the Class Observation form (Appendix A, page 105).

Another concern focuses on the texts students read. We want students to choose texts at an appropriate level, in this case texts they will be able to read with ease. How can we be sure that this will occur? We need to work with students to establish some text selection guidelines. I can think of four ways to teach children how to select texts. These are shown in Figure 10.1.

What of those children who will undoubtedly reread? Perhaps this is not the problem we think it is. Thinking back to my music example, I often took familiar songs with me into the practice room so that I could practice vocal techniques. The same can be said for readers who choose easy texts during independent silent reading time. Through this practice, they can gain much in the way of developing a sight vocabulary and other skills associated with fluency, such as appropriate speed, word identification, and prosody. And let's face it: it's fun to reread a familiar text!

A third concern centers on time on task. I do not need any formal research findings (although there are several) to prove to me that struggling readers can be the best at practicing avoidance behaviors when it comes to reading. I've watched struggling readers make it look as though they are reading by browsing through books or some other texts such as magazines when all they are doing is turning the pages. Fortunately, there is much we can do to help students overcome these avoidance behaviors and replace them with real reading. For instance, we can create text baskets of texts at specific reading levels and instruct children to choose from an appropriate basket. We can also have children create a basket for themselves at the start of the week and have them use this basket during independent silent reading. And, as noted in Step 6, we can provide students with a variety of texts that are sure to capture their interest. Finally, we

FIGURE 10.1

Teaching Children How to Select Texts

Technique	*Explanation*
1. Have a whole-class meeting and encourage children to generate criteria. List the criteria on a chart large enough for all to see. You might also want to divide the list into three categories: On the Easy Side, Just Right, and On the Hard Side.	Involving students in determining the criteria helps them to better understand what it is they need to look for. Once the list of criteria has been generated, post it and encourage the class to refer to it when selecting texts.
2. Explain to students how to use the "thumb test": • Open the book to the middle. • Open up your right or left hand. • Read a page of the book to yourself. • Beginning with your little finger, put one finger down every time you come to a word you don't know. If you finish the page and your thumb is still up, you probably have a text that is good for you.	This test has been around for quite some time (Veatch, 1968) and has proven helpful for many students.
3. Provide children with a list of questions.	Use the questions shown in Figure 10.2 or design some of your own.
4. Read aloud parts of different texts.	By reading aloud different kinds of texts, you can help children see that there are many good texts aside from those they may consider all-time favorites. By moving beyond the familiar, students read more types of books with many different text structures.

Don't Speed. READ!

FIGURE 10.2

Questions for Readers

Easy Texts

Ask yourself these questions. If you circle Yes, this text is probably an easy one for you.

1. Have you read it before?	Yes	No
2. Can you read it without stumbling?	Yes	No
3. Can you tell the ideas to someone else?	Yes	No

Just-Right Texts

Ask yourself these questions. If you circle Yes, this text is probably just right for you.

1. Have you read it before?	Yes	No
2. Can you read most words?	Yes	No
3. Can you tell the ideas to someone else?	Yes	No
4. Could you read this text if you had a little help?	Yes	No

Challenge Texts

Ask yourself these questions. If you circle No to 1 and 2 and Yes to 3 and 4, this text is probably going to be a little difficult for you.

1. Have you read it before?	Yes	No
2. Can you read most words?	Yes	No
3. Does the text confuse you?	Yes	No
4. Would you need a lot of help to read it?	Yes	No

can develop a list of guidelines with students so that they will know exactly what needs to happen during independent silent reading.

Atwell (2007) provides a list of rules that she and her students follow for reading workshop. I've adapted this list for independent silent reading:

Rules for Independent Silent Reading

1. You must read some type of text, such as books, magazines, or comic books.

2. If you select something that you don't like, stop reading it and choose something else to read. Remember that you're trying to keep reading the entire time.

3. You can read a text more than one time if you want.

4. You need to keep a list of everything you read during independent reading time, even if you did not finish it. Use the form in your independent reading folder.

5. Read the entire reading time and read as much as you can.

As you can see, independent silent reading demands much responsibility, not to mention structure. It is anything but a free-for-all in which students are allowed to do whatever they want. It is a deliberate, planned time of the day with a definite purpose. As students read, we busy ourselves observing students and making notations about what we see. At other times, we keep students focused on reading. At still other times, we help students read a text. And if we are lucky, there are times when we get to read something for ourselves!

REFLECTION

Take some time to think and talk with your colleagues about how you currently use independent silent reading. Here are some questions to facilitate your thinking:

- How do you structure it?

- Now that you have read this step, is there any way you might modify how you use independent silent reading?

- How much time do you allot for independent silent reading? Do you increase the time over the school year?

Communicate With Families

"That one, again?" the father asks his five-year-old son. Smiling, the child nods yes, and the reading aloud of a favorite book begins. As much as the father might want to offer a short-cut version by skipping a few pages here and there, he knows that doing so will not work. The child knows the book all too well and will take him back to missed pages or will interrupt the reading by stating something like, "Hey! You forgot to read the part about . . . ." Instead, the father will most likely read the book differently than he did the night before so that he can stay interested and convey a sense of enjoyment. He might use his voice in different ways (prosody), read some parts more quickly than others (speed), and exaggerate punctuation markings (prosody). He might pause to see if his son can state a word before he does (accuracy). He might laugh at parts he finds humorous. He might even ask his son a few questions now and then (comprehension).

What's going on here has much to do with teaching a child about reading fluency, although the father, assuming that he is not an educator and knows little about specific ways of teaching fluency, may be unaware of how his actions are teaching his son about all three elements of reading fluency: speed, accuracy, and prosody. Instead, he focuses on enjoying the story with his son and *showing* rather than *telling* his son the value of reading. He may not fully realize the effects of his reading aloud to his son in this manner: He is increasing the odds that his son will read with fluency and have a positive attitude toward reading (Lancy & Bergin, 1992).

And perhaps this is as it should be. After all, if parents are reading to their children and providing them with a print-rich environment, do they really need to know as much as we educators know about what specific skills they are engendering in their children? Can't we just leave them alone so that they will keep their energy focused on reading for enjoyment and making time for reading a daily priority?

For some, I think we can. These are the parents who seem to be naturals with reading. In other words, they just seem to know what to do with their children when they read aloud to them even though they might not be able to put an educator's label on what they are doing. My wife, an insurance-premium auditor, is a perfect example. On occasion, I would watch her read to our youngest son and marvel at how she would stop at just the right spots that would encourage prediction. What's more, she would read with expression, changing her voice to signal different characters, and pause at the end of a page, signaling that it needed to be turned and wait for him to turn it. She never attended a teacher education program, but watching her read aloud would have you believe otherwise. On one such occasion, I asked her if she knew all of the great reading skills she was teaching our son by reading to him the way she did. Her look said it all but she also delivered a verbal punch, "Can't you ever just read a book for some fun and enjoyment? Why do you always have to think about what skills are being taught?"

Long an advocate of parental involvement and providing parents with concrete ideas about how to help their children become better readers, I found that her questions made me rethink the whole idea of parental involvement. I realized that there are parents like her who provide a variety of reading opportunities for their children. Most of these parents already *unconsciously* know how to read to their children. They don't need to attend a special training session to watch a video that shows them how to do so (e.g., how to hold the book, how to seat your child so that both of you can see the book with ease). Most of these parents value education so much that they monitor what their children are doing in school. They are involved in numerous ways. For example, not only do they read with and to their children, they also make sure that time is allotted for other homework. These are the parents who respond to notes sent home from school and attend parent-teacher conferences. Many of these are parents who have positive feelings about school because of their own schooling experiences. They are not afraid to approach teachers or to show up at school unannounced. In fact, these parents are so comfortable with the whole schooling experience that they are open to learning. Given a specific reading technique such as paired reading, coupled with an understanding of how to use it, they will cooperate with teachers and use it in the best interests of their children.

I also understand that there are many parents who are just the opposite. When it comes to reading to their children or fostering a literacy-rich environment, they may not be natural teachers. They need some help in learning how to engage with their children. Even though they may not be as comfortable with the school setting, most are willing to learn specific ways to help their children become better readers. I have discovered what I suspect many of you know as well about the best ways to enlist the support of these parents: They need activities that are easy to understand and use and they need them one at a time rather than all at once. They also need to be supplied with all materials (e.g., texts) to complete an activity so that they do not have to fret over whether they have selected the best possible texts for their children to read. Finally, the activities need to focus on reading for enjoyment and on reading for meaning. After a long day at work, these parents, like all parents, are tired. They want to engage with their children in fun rather than arduous activities.

Whether they are naturals or not, here's the big idea about including parents.

Parental involvement is essential to maximize their children's reading potential, including reading fluency (Darling & Westberg, 2004; Epstein, 1991; Paris, Wasik, & Turner, 1991; Postlewaite & Ross, 1992; Snow, Burns, & Griffin, 1998; Wasik, 2004).

But just how to involve parents always seems to present a challenge. For example, if we invite parents to come to evening meetings, several may not show for one reason or another. I suppose that one reason for their lack of attendance is that like most of us who get home after working all day, the last idea that we would entertain after getting dinner ready and served, tidying the kitchen, and making sure that the children are doing their chores and homework, is finding a sitter so that we can leave home for a parent meeting at school. It isn't that they don't want to learn what the meeting is designed to teach. It's just that there are other more pressing issues.

There are numerous other challenges, including working with parents who are challenged readers and writers themselves and those whose first language isn't English (Bohler, Eichenlaub, Litteken, & Wallis, 1996). The good news is that recognizing the challenges puts us in a better position to help them. If we sense that we are working with low-literate parents, for example, we can use telephone calls rather than a printed newsletter to communicate with them. If we are working with parents whose first language is not English, we can seek out people to help us communicate with them in their first language (see Freeman & Freeman, 2007, for specific suggestions). If we are working with parents who are unlikely to leave home for an evening school meeting primarily because they cannot afford to hire a babysitter, we can structure the meetings so that their children can accompany them and, indeed, become essential participants themselves.

Take, for example, an experience I once had as a university professor. A local school district curriculum coordinator called me about conducting a parent session. She wanted me to show parents how to use paired reading. After giving this idea much thought and considering my past experiences with trying to involve parents, I decided that I would conduct the meeting *if* the children could accompany their parents. I further stated that the children would need to be included for some but not all of the meeting. When the children were not taking part, they would need to be brought to another room in the school and supervised. As luck would have it, the curriculum coordinator's son was a Boy Scout. She enlisted him and the rest of his troop to supervise the children.

Here's how the meeting played out. I initiated the meeting with everyone in the room. After introductions and an explanation of the agenda, the Boy Scouts ushered the children out of the room and took them to other classrooms in the school where they read stories to and with the children. Then, I provided the parents with a detailed

FIGURE 11.1

Fluency Activities and Brief Descriptions

Name of Activity	Brief Description
Echo Reading	The parent reads aloud a segment of text while the child follows along. The child then rereads the same segment.
Choral Reading	The parent and child read a text in unison.
Read-Aloud	The parent selects and practices a book to read aloud with specific emphases in mind.
Partner Reading	In some manner, the parent and child read a text together. There are many variations of this procedure, as described in Appendix B.
Neurological Impress	The parent sits alongside the child and reads into the child's ear while the child also reads aloud.
Reading While Listening	The child reads silently while listening to the parent read the text aloud, modeling proficient reading. There are many variations to this procedure, as described in Appendix B.
Closed-Captioned Television	The sound is turned off and the captions are turned on. The child then watches and reads a given television show.

---

explanation of paired reading and handouts to remind them of the steps. I then had them practice with one another. The Boy Scouts brought the children back into the room and guided them to the tables where I had displayed several books, magazines, and comics. The children were given time to select a text to read with their parents. Once each child had found a text to read, I had the parents practice doing paired reading with their children. After about ten minutes, I asked the Boy Scouts to take the children out of the room again so that I could talk with the parents about how their paired reading sessions went and answer any questions they might have about it. Finally, the children and parents were reunited in the cafeteria for refreshments. All of the participants agreed that the meeting was a huge success in terms of turnout and parents' facility with the technique.

Yes, I know. This example, as well as others that you might encounter in your professional reading (e.g. the Family Fluency Program described by Morrow, Kuhn, & Shwanenflugel, 2006) require a tremendous amount of energy on the part of the classroom teacher. In fact, it takes several individuals working together to make events such as these successful. And as exhilarating as they can be, they tend to be few and far between because we simply do not have the time to put them together. And I am not suggesting that we should. My main point is that there are no simple answers to the challenges we face when working with parents. We have to persist if we are serious about including parents and we have to be willing to try different ideas. As with anything that we truly value, we will find a way to make it work.

The seven activities I list in Figure 11.1 and describe in detail in Appendix B can be completed at home with relative ease. All seven will help children further develop reading fluency, not to mention other essential components of reading, such as comprehension and developing a positive attitude toward reading.

You are now in a better position to get parents involved. To better ensure parents' success with these activities, I offer a couple of reminders:

• Rather than overwhelm parents by providing them with a list of these activities, provide them with one idea and include the text you want to have them read with their children. You might think about putting both the explanation and the text in an envelope along with any other materials they might need for the activity. Your explanation might take the form of a friendly letter such as the one in Figure 11.2.

• Keep your communication as jargon-free as possible. Notice in the sample letter shown in Figure 11.2 that I focus on what I want parents to do with their children rather than providing them with many labels. Reading in phrases is one aspect of prosody, which is one component of reading fluency. Do parents need to know that? I don't think so. Will trying to explain this terminology to parents enhance their ability to help their children? I don't think so. Will launching into an explanation such as this shut many parents down? I think it will.

• Remember that most parents are at a loss when it comes to knowing which text or texts they should have their children read. They need help. One way to help them is to provide them with a specific text to use with the activity you send home, rather than a list of many titles. Sending home the actual text you want parents and their children to use allows them to focus on the activity rather than using that time to round up the text. Consider providing parents with specific Web sites that will enable them to identify appropriate texts and ways to help their children without having to leave home (assuming that they have Internet access at home). Again, rather than providing them with one big list, I suggest providing them with one site at a time, perhaps with a sample page printed out from the site.

FIGURE 11.2

Sample Letter to Parents

Dear Parents,

One skill your children have been practicing is reading in phrases. Because poetry is written using phrases, I have been having children select poems and practice reading them silently before asking them to read the poem aloud to an interested audience. Here's where I need your help. I have included a poem for your child to practice reading at home. I ask that you do the following:

1. Read the poem to yourself so that you are comfortable reading it.
2. Read the poem aloud to your child. Point out to your child how you read the words in phrases rather than by using choppy word-by-word reading.
3. Have your child read the poem with you.
4. Finally, have your child practice reading the poem once or twice.
5. In the space below the poem, please sign your name. Your signature means that you completed the reading with your child.

Thank you for your willingness to help your child become a better reader by reading and rereading this poem.

Sincerely,
Your child's teacher

Fortunately, there are many Web sites now available for parents and children. Some of these are created by educators for their school districts; others are created by professional organizations and publishers. Here are just a few:

Web Sites for Parents

PROFESSIONAL ORGANIZATIONS:

www.nea.org/parents/index.html (National Education Association)

www.reading.org (International Reading Association)

Both of these sites offer numerous suggestions for ways that parents can get involved in their children's reading education. Specific book titles for different ages and interests are also provided.

PUBLISHERS:
www.scholastic.com/families/index.asp (Scholastic)
www.sfreading (Scott Foresman)
Each of these provides appropriate grade-level books and activities sure to be helpful to most families.

GOVERNMENT:
www.ed.gov/parents/academic/help/reader/index.html
www.ed.gov/pubs/parents/writing/index.html
Both of these Department of Education Web pages offer several ideas and publications for all ages and stages of growth.

OTHER
www.rif.org (Reading Is Fundamental)
www.familyeducation.com (Family Education)
www.vsarts.org (VSA Arts)
These Web sites offer suggestions for reading-related activities as well as other important information.

Web Sites for Children
www.umass.edu/Aesop (Offers Aesop's fables)
pbskids.org/arthur/ (Offers Marc Brown's Arthur)
www.magickeys.com/books/ (Offers a children's storybook online)
www.guysread.com (Offers suggestions especially appealing to boys)
www.dustbunny.com (Offers astronomy for children)
A number of children's authors, such as Mem Fox, Jan Brett, Eric Carle, and Janet Stevens, also have Web sites that children might find interesting.

→ REFLECTION →

Where do you think you will begin? Which of these activities do you think will work best for the parents and children you serve? Which have you already tried and modified to better fit your needs? Which Web sites can you see yourself using? How might they connect with specific activities? Take some time to reflect on these questions and write notes in the chart on the next page. As with the other reflections, talking with interested colleagues is sure to provide even more insights.

FLUENCY ACTIVITIES YOU CAN SHARE WITH FAMILIES

Activity	Comments
Echo Reading	
Choral Reading	
Read-Aloud	
Partner Reading	
Neurological Impress	
Reading While Listening	
Closed-Captioned Television	

12

Keep It Simple!

Given the previous 11 steps and their accompanying explanations, you might think that focusing the last step on simplicity is an oxymoron. And I suppose in some ways it is. As with any instruction we design, there are many considerations to think through in our efforts to teach fluency effectively. This being said, I do think there are some ways that we can make it easier for our students and ourselves, hence the hint of simplicity. In closing this book, then, I offer the following suggestions.

Use the known to teach the unknown.

When we use what children already know to teach them something they need to know to grow as readers, we are teaching from a position of strength. This kind of teaching helps children make meaningful associations between their current knowledge and the knowledge they are acquiring. The result is that they better understand what they have been taught and can better apply it when reading.

Take, for example, second- or third-grade children who read word by word primarily out of habit. While there are times when we all tend to slow our reading down and read word by word (e.g., when I was following written directions to put together a tin storage shed I purchased at a "bargain price"), most often we read in phrases. It keeps our thoughts moving, and it's more efficient. It also helps us to better understand the text.

Let's say that you recognize that poetry provides one of the best ways to teach phrasing because most poets use meaningful phrases. Let's also assume that you firmly believe that teaching from the known to the unknown will better help children acquire new understandings. Guided by these understandings, you design and teach the following lesson.

To prepare for the lesson, you secure a poem that has been written with one word on each line. Two examples are "I Live for Gym" by Kali Dakos and "Night" by Lamm. You secure another poem that has been written with phrases on each line. Two examples are Dakos's "I'd Mark With the Sunshine" and Douglas Florian's "Handsprings." You then enlarge each poem for all to see and display them side by side.

To open the lesson, you ask children to look at both poems and to tell what they see. Some children may notice that there is one word per line on the first poem and two, three, or four words on each line of the second poem. If they do not, you call attention to this feature by saying something like "The poet who wrote this first poem decided to put one word on each line and the other poet decided to put more than one word on each line."

The lesson proceeds as you then read the first poem to the children while they follow along. You point out that you had to read word by word because that is how the poem is written. You also say something such as "I have noticed that many of you read word by word and that is the perfect way to read a poem like this one. Read it with me this time." You then have children join you in a repeated reading of the poem.

After the reading, you continue, "Word-by-word reading really works for poems like this, but most of the time, readers usually group words together into phrases. Let's practice with a different poem. I'll read it first while you follow along. Then you can read it with me. If you are not used to reading in groups of words, you might feel a little uncomfortable. This is a natural feeling. The more you practice reading in phrases, the more comfortable you will become."

You then read the second poem as they follow along. You point out that you had to read the words in phrases or chunks for the poem to make sense because that is how this poem is written. As readers, we take our cues on how to read the poem from the author. You then have children join you in two or three repeated readings of this poem so that they can gain some comfort and confidence with reading in phrases.

You conclude the lesson saying something like "So now you have had some practice reading in phrases. Today during independent silent reading time, select another poem and practice reading in phrases or try reading in phrases with the text you are currently reading. Remember that the most important part of reading is understanding what you read, and reading in phrases can often help you do just that. "

Keep it real.

As a result of my own teaching experiences, university level included, and my experiences as a learner, I am convinced that in order for a lesson to have any lasting effect, its content must be meaningful to learners. Learners need to be able to make some meaningful associations. If, they cannot, little learning occurs. Think of the times when you attend staff development sessions. If you connect with the content and see how you might be able to use it to better your teaching and students' learning, you are most likely very attentive. If, on the other hand, you don't, you are most likely less attentive and happy when the session is complete. Your only satisfaction comes from having survived another mundane session.

I think the same is true with children. For instance, take children who are taught "fluency" in kindergarten. Most can make few if any meaningful associations with the explicit fluency lessons because they are not ready for this kind of instruction. In the words of two researchers who conducted an analysis of fluency studies (Kuhn & Stahl, 2000), "Fluency instruction seems to work best with children between a late pre-primer level and late second-grade level" (p. 23). Moskal and Blachowicz (2006) also note the appropriateness of starting explicit fluency instruction in second grade. Children need to have acquired some words that they know by sight and they need to be able to read connected text. Most kindergarten children have yet to acquire the necessary reading vocabulary.

Their findings do not negate the value of the informal kind of fluency instruction that I mention in Step 5 and in Step 8. But the focus is on helping kindergartners understand and use oral language fluently as a segue into doing the same with printed materials. Kindergarten teachers who use poem charts, song charts, big books, and the like are helping children develop fluency even though they might not call explicit attention to appropriate speed, accuracy, or prosody. They show these features through their actions.

And how about the children who have difficulty with phrasing for one reason or another?

Assuming that the primary reason is out of habit, I can think of no better way to teach phrasing than by first engaging children with poetry as previously described. I fear that giving children "parsed text" (Fox, 2003), text that has been marked with slash marks to indicate phrases within a paragraph and two slash marks to signal the end of a sentence, will confuse their understanding rather than assist it, especially if they are given this type of text when they are first trying to understand and apply phrasing in their own reading. I also grow concerned when these children are given text and told to parse it themselves. If they can do so, it would appear to me that they already know how to phrase and that they don't require this kind of instruction. If, on the other hand, they do not appear to phrase when they read, how can we expect them to parse the text? I fear that they will take wild guesses, perhaps counting words in threes and making slashes to accomplish the activity without understanding what it is they are attempting to learn. Finally, parsing text simply does not help those who struggle the most with fluency (Young & Grieg, 1995).

Integrate it!

Remember that what we want children to understand is that there are many proficient reader behaviors that cut across all content areas (see Step 8 for a list of proficient reading behaviors). Any time they are reading, these behaviors kick in. Fluency is but one of these behaviors. We can best help children with this understanding and save ourselves a lot of time by integrating any needed fluency instruction within our current framework, as I make clear in Step 9.

Consider using every step.

If you are like me, you did not read this book from front to back. Instead, you did what I usually do. I flip through the book, skim the table of contents, take a look at the index, and first read the chapters that appeal to me the most. I then return to the other chapters to get a sense of the text as a whole. Regardless of the order in which you read the steps, you now have a sense of each. You also know that every step is important. How can you design fluency instruction, for example, if you do not know what fluency means? How can you choose specific fluency activities if you haven't assessed your students' needs? How can you involve parents if you aren't sure what it is you are trying to accomplish?

→ REFLECTION →

Clearly, there is much to think through in an effort to provide the best possible instruction. Perhaps one of the best ways to think through each step is to use the self-assessment guide below. You may want to return to each step as you consider it.

Teacher Self-Assessment Guide for 12 Fluency Steps

Step	Statement	Yes	No	Thoughts/Ideas
1	I have thought through my definition of fluency.			
2	My definition of fluency fits with my view on how children acquire reading.			
3	My fluency assessment techniques coincide with my definition of fluency.			
4	I use student self-assessment.			

Step	Statement	Yes	No	Thoughts/Ideas
5	I select appropriate fluency activities to accomplish a given objective and group children accordingly.			
6	I use a variety of texts to help children become more-fluent readers.			
7	I have established a nurturing environment in which all children can thrive.			
8	I have a written plan that shows how I will explicitly teach something about fluency.			
9	I provide time for independent silent reading for every student.			
10	I integrate fluency instruction with other content areas.			
11	I regularly communicate with parents, giving them specific suggestions for ways they can help further their children's reading growth.			
12	I deliberately find ways to keep fluency instruction simple and meaningful.			

References

Allington, R. (1983). Fluency: The neglected goal. *The Reading Teacher, 36*: 556–561.

Allington, R. (2006). *What really matters for struggling readers: Designing research-based programs* (2nd ed.). New York: Pearson Allyn & Bacon.

Almasi, J., McKeown, M., & Beck, I. (1996). The nature of engaged reading in classroom discussions of literature. *Journal of Literacy Research, 28*(1), 107–146.

Anderson, R. (1996). Research foundations to support wide reading. In V. Greaney (Ed.) *Promoting reading in developing countries* (pp. 55–77). Newark, DE: International Reading Association.

Applegate, M., Quinn, K., & Applegate, A. (2004). *The critical reading inventory.* Upper Saddle River, NJ: Merrill/Prentice Hall.

Atwell, N. (2007). *The reading zone.* New York: Scholastic.

Betts, E. (1946). *Foundations of reading instruction.* New York: American Book Company.

Blachowicz, C., Sullivan, D., & Cieply, C. (2001). Fluency snapshots: A quick screening tool for your classroom. *Reading Psychology, 22*, 95–109.

Brecht, R. (1977). Testing format and instructional level with the informal reading inventory. *The Reading Teacher, 31*, 57–59.

Brown, J., Goodman, K., & Marek, A. (1996). *Studies in miscue analysis: An annotated bibliography.* Newark, DE: International Reading Association.

Cambourne, B. (1995). Towards an educationally relevant theory of literacy learning: Twenty years of inquiry. *The Reading Teacher, 49*, 182–202.

Clay, M. (1991). Introducing a new storybook to young readers. *The Reading Teacher, 45,* 264–73.

Clay, M. (1983). *The early detection of reading difficulties.* Portsmouth, NH: Heinemann.

Cooter, R., Flynt, E. S., & Cooter, K. (2007). *Comprehensive reading inventory.* Columbus, OH: Pearson/Merrill/Prentice Hall.

Darling, S. & Westberg, L. (2004). Parent involvement in children's acquisition of reading. *The Reading Teacher, 57,* 774–776.

Duffy, G. (2003). *Explaining reading: A resource for teaching concepts, skills, and strategies.* New York: Guilford.

Durkin, D. (1990). *Teaching them to read* (6th ed.). New York: Pearson Allyn & Bacon.

Epstein, J. (1991). Effects on student achievement of teachers' practices of parent involvement. *Advances in Reading/Language Research, 5,* 261–276.

Flurkey, A. (2006). What's "normal" about real reading? In K. Goodman (Ed.), *The truth about DIBELS: What it is and what it does* (pp. 40–49). Portsmouth, NH: Heinemann.

Fox, B. (2003). *Word recognition activities: Patterns and strategies for developing fluency.* Upper Saddle River, NJ: Merrill.

Freeman, D. & Freeman, Y. (2007). *English language learners: The essential guide.* New York: Scholastic.

Goforth, F. (1998). *Literature & the learner*. Belmont, CA: Wadsworth.

Goodman, K. (2006). A critical review of DIBELS. In K. Goodman (Ed.), *The truth about DIBELS: What it is and what it does* (pp. 1–39). Portsmouth, NH: Heinemann.

Guthrie, J., Wigfield, A., Metsala, J., & Cox, K. (1999). Motivational and cognitive predictors of text comprehension and reading amount. *Sceintific Studies of Reading, 3*, 231–256.

Halliday, M. (1975). *Explorations in the functions of language*. London: Arnold.

Harris, A., & Sipay, E. (1990). *How to increase reading ability: A guide to developmental and remedial methods*. New York: Longman.

Harris, T., & Hodges, R. (1995). *The literacy dictionary: The vocabulary of reading and writing*. Newark, DE: International Reading Association.

Hasbrouck, J., & Tindal, G. (2006). Oral reading fluency norms: A valuable assessment tool for reading teachers. *The Reading Teacher, 59*, 636–644.

Herber, H. (1978). *Teaching reading in content areas* (2nd ed.). Englewood Cliffs, NJ: Prentice Hall.

Hiebert, E. (2006). Becoming fluent: Repeated reading with scaffolded texts. In S. J. Samuels & A. Fargstrup (Eds.), *What research has to say about fluency instruction* (pp. 204–226). Newark, DE: International Reading Association.

International Reading Association. (1998). *Learning to read and write: Developmentally appropriate practices for young children: A joint position statement of the International Reading Association and the National Association for the Education of Young Children*. Newark, DE: International Reading Association.

Johns, J., & Berglund, R. (2006). *Fluency strategies and assessments* (2nd ed.). Newark, DE: International Reading Association.

Kamil, M., Kim, H., & Lane, D. (2004). Electronic text in the classroom. In J. Hoffman & D. Schallert (Eds.), *The texts in elementary classrooms* (pp. 157–193). Mahwah, NJ: Erlbaum.

Karp, M. (1943). Silent before oral reading. *Elementary School Journal, 44*(2), 102–104.

Kohn, A. (1996). *Beyond discipline: From compliance to community*. Alexandria, VA: Association for Supervision and Curriculum Development.

Krashen, S. (2004). *The power of reading: Insights from the research* (2nd ed.). Portsmouth, NH: Heinemann.

Kucer, S. (2005). *The dimensions of literacy: A conceptual base for teaching reading and writing in school settings* (2nd ed.). Mahwah, NJ: Erlbaum.

Kuhn, M., & Stahl, S. (2000). *Fluency: A review of developmental and remedial practices* (CIERA Report #2-008). Ann Arbor, MI: University of Michigan, Center for the Improvement of Early Reading Achievement.

Lancy, D.F., & Bergin, C. (1992, April). *The role of parents in supporting beginning reading*. Paper presented at the annual meeting of the American Educational Research Association, San Francisco, CA.

Linehart, G., Zigmond, N., & Cooley, W. (1981). Reading instruction and its effects. *American Educational Research Journal, 18*, 343–361.

Manning, G., & Manning, M. (1984). What models of recreational reading make a difference? *Reading World, 23*(4), 375–380.

Morrow, L., Kuhn, M., & Schwanenflugel, P. (2006). The family fluency program. *The Reading Teacher, 60*(4), 322–333.

Moskal, M., & Blachowicz, C. (2006). *Partnering for fluency.* New York: Guilford.

National Institute for Literacy. (2000). *Report of the National Reading Panel. Teaching children to read: Reports of the subgroups* (NIH Publication no. 00-4754). Washington, DC: U.S. Government Printing Office.

National Institute of Child Health and Human Development (NICHD). (2000). *Report of the National Reading Panel. Teaching children to read: Reports of the subgroups* (NIH Publication no. 00-4754). Washington, DC: U.S. Government Printing Office.

Opitz, M. (1998). *Flexible grouping in reading.* New York: Scholastic.

Opitz, M., & Ford, M. (2001). *Reaching readers: Flexible and innovative strategies for guided reading.* Portsmouth, NH: Heinemann.

Opitz, M., & Ford, M. (2006). *Books and beyond: New ways to reach readers.* Portsmouth, NH: Heinemann.

Opitz, M., & Rasinski, T. (1998). *Good-bye round robin: 25 effective oral reading strategies.* Portsmouth, NH: Heinemann.

Paris, S., & Carpenter, R. (2004). *The texts in elementary classrooms.* New York: Guilford.

Paris, S., Wasik, B., & Turner, J. (1991). The development of strategic readers. In R. Barr, M. Kamil, P. Mosenthal, & P. D. Pearson (Eds.), *Handbook of reading research,* (Vol. 2, pp. 609–640). New York: Longman.

Peterson, B. (1991). Selecting books for beginning readers and children's literature suitable for young readers. In D. DeFord, C. Lyons, & G. Pinnell (Eds.), *Bridges to literacy: Learning from reading recovery* (pp. 119–147). Portsmouth, NH: Heinemann.

Pikulski, J. (2006). Fluency: A developmental and language perspective. In S. J. Samuels & A. Fargstrup (Eds.), *What research has to say about fluency instruction* (pp. 70–93). Newark, DE: International Reading Association.

Postlewaite, T., & Ross, K. (1992). *Effective schools in reading: Implications for educational planners.* The Hague, the Netherlands: International Association for the Evaluation of Educational Achievement.

Pressley, M., Allington, R., Wharton-MacDonald, R., Block, C., & Morrow, L. (2001). *Learning to read: Lessons from exemplary first-grade classrooms.* New York: Guilford.

Pressley, M., Gaskins, I., & Fingeret, L. (2006). Instruction and development of reading fluency in struggling readers. In S. J. Samuels & A. Fargstrup (Eds.), *What research has to say about fluency instruction* (pp. 47–69). Newark, DE: International Reading Association.

Pressley, M., Hilden, K., & Shankland, R. (2005). *An evaluation of end-grade-3 Dynamic Indicators of Basic Early Literacy Skills (DIBELS): Speed reading without comprehension, predicting little* (technical report). East Lansing, MI: Literacy Achievement Research Center.

Rasinski, T., & Padak, N. (2004). *3-Minute reading assessments: Word recognition, fluency, and comprehension.* New York: Scholastic.

Rayner, K., & Pollastek, A. (1994). *The psychology of reading.* Hillsdale, NJ: Erlbaum.

Reutzel, D. R. (2006). "Hey, teacher, when you say 'fluency,' what do you mean?" Developing fluency in elementary classrooms. In T. Rasinski, C. Blachowicz, & K. Lems (Eds.), *Fluency instruction: research-based practices* (pp. 62–85). New York: Guilford.

Reutzel, D. R., & Hollingsworth, P. (1991). Investigating topic-related attitude: Effect on reading and remembering text. *Journal of Educational Research, 84*(6), 334–344.

Rubin, D., & Opitz, M. (2007). *Diagnosis and improvement of reading instruction* (5th ed.). New York: Pearson Allyn & Bacon.

Samuels, S. J. (1979). The method of repeated readings. *The Reading Teacher, 32,* 403–408.

Samuels, S. J. (2006). Toward a model of reading fluency. In S. J. Samuels & A. Fargstrup (Eds.), *What research has to say about fluency instruction* (pp. 24–46). Newark, DE: International Reading Association.

Samuels, S. J., & Fargstrup, A. (2006). Reading fluency instruction: Will it be a passing fad or permanent fixture? In S. J. Samuels & A. Fargstrup (Eds.), *What research has to say about fluency instruction* (pp. 1–3). Newark, DE: International Reading Association.

Schwanenflugel, P., Kuhn, M., Strauss, G., & Morris, R. (2006). Becoming a fluent and automatic reader in the early elementary school years. *Reading Research Quarterly, 41*(4), 496–522.

Snow, C., Burns, M., & Griffin, P. (1998). *Preventing reading difficulties in young children.* Washington DC: National Academy Press.

Strang, R. (1969). *Diagnostic teaching of reading* (2nd ed.). New York: McGraw-Hill.

U.S. Department of Education. Institute of Education Sciences. National Center for Education Statistics. *The Nation's Report Card: Reading 2002*, NCES 2003–521, by W. S. Grigg, M. C. Daane, Y. Jin, and J. R. Campbell. Washington, DC: 2003.

Veatch, J. (1968). *How to teach reading with children's books.* New York: RC Owne.

Walczyk, J., & Griffith-Ross, D. (2007). How important is reading skill fluency for comprehension? *The Reading Teacher, 60*, 560–569.

Wasik, B. (2004). *Handbook of family literacy.* Mahwah, NJ: Erlbaum.

Wharton-McDonald, R., Pressley, M., & Hampston, J. (1998). Literacy instruction in nine first-grade classrooms: Teacher characteristics and student achievement. *Elementary School Journal, 99*, 101–128.

Winn, B., Skinner, C., Oliver, R., Hale, A., & Ziegler, M. (2006). The effects of listening while reading and repeated reading on the reading fluency of adult learners. *Journal of Adolescent and Adult Literacy, 50*(3), 196–205.

Young, A., & Grieg, P. (1995). Individual difference and text difficulty determinants of reading fluency and expressiveness. *Journal of Experimental Child Psychology, 60*, 428–454.

Zargota, N. (1997). *Rethinking language arts: Passion and practice.* New York: Guilford.

Children's Texts Cited

Song Texts

A-Tisket, a-Tasket by Ella Fitzgerald (Philomel, 2003)

America the Beautiful by Katherine L. Bates (Putnam, 2003)

Don't Laugh at Me by Steve Seskin & Allen Sahmblin (Tricycle, 2002)

Here We Go Round the Mulberry Bush by Will Hillenbrand (Harcourt, 2003)

Skip to My Lou by Mary Ann Hoberman & Nadine Bernard Westcott (Little Brown, 2003)

Poetry Texts

Block City by Robert Louis Stevenson (Simon & Schuster, 2005)

Down to the Sea in Ships by Philemon Sturges (Putnam, 2005)

Handsprings by Douglas Florian (Greenwillow, 2006)

In the Swim by Douglas Florian (Harcourt, 1997)

School Supplies: A Book of Poems by Lee Bennett Hopkins (Simon & Schuster, 1996)

When I Heard the Learn'd Astronomer by Walt Whitman (Simon & Schuster, 2004)

Predictable Books

The Deep Blue Sea: A Book of Colors by Audrey Wood (Scholastic, 2005)

Good Morning, Digger by Anne Rockwell (Viking, 2005)

One Red Dot by David A. Carter (Simon & Schuster, 2005)

Mommies Say Shhh! by Patricia Polacco (Philomel, 2005)

Why Not? by Mary Wormell (Farrar, Straus & Giroux, 2000)

Nonfiction Texts

Baby Sea Otter by Betty Tatham (Holt, 2005)

Into the Ice: The Story of Arctic Exploration by Lynn Curlee (Houghton Mifflin, 1998)

Liberty Rising: The Story of the Statue of Liberty by Pegi Deitz Shea (Holt, 2005)

On Earth by G. Brian Karas (Putnam, 2005)

Multilevel Books

Elephants Can Paint, Too by Katya Arnold (Simon & Schuster, 2005)

Sharks and Other Dangers of the Deep by Simon Mugford (St. Martin's, 2005)

A Subway for New York by David Weitzman (Farrar, Straus & Giroux, 2005)

This Rocket by Paul Collicutt (Farrar, Straus, & Giroux, 2005)

Wise Guy: The Life and Philosophy of Socrates by M. D. Usher (Farrar, Straus, & Giroux, 2005)

Series Books

Cam Jansen by David A. Adler (Scholastic)

Gus and Grandpa by Claudia Mills (Farrar, Straus, & Giroux)

Hank, the Cowdog by John R. Erickson (Viking)
Harry Potter by J. K. Rowling (Scholastic)
Polk Street Kids by Patricia Reilly Giff (Doubleday)
The Zack Files by Dan Greenburg (Grosset & Dunlap)

Chapter Books

Frog and Toad series by Arnold Lobel (Harper & Row)
Henry and Mudge series by Cynthia Rylant (Aladdin)
Bud, Not Buddy by Christopher Paul Curtis (Delacorte, 1999)
The Giver by Lois Lowry (Houghton Mifflin, 1993)
Missing May by Cynthia Rylant (Yearling, 1993)
Shiloh by Phyllis Naylor (Aladdin, 2000)
Walk Two Moons by Sharon Creech (HarperTrophy, 1994)

Texts That Include Scripts

Frog Went A-Courting by Dominic Catalano (Boyds Mills Press, 1998)
Replay by Sharon Creech (Joanna Colter, 2005)
What's the Time, Grandma Wolf? by Ken Brown (Peachtree, 2001)
You're On! Seven Plays in English and Spanish by Lori Marie Carlson (Morrow Junior Books, 1999)

Magazines

Cricket Magazine (Carus)
Sesame Street Magazine (Sesame Street)
Zoobooks (Wildlife Education)

Newspapers

Weekly Reader (Boyds Mills Press)
Scholastic News (Scholastic)

Basal Readers

Treasures (McGraw-Hill, 2005)
Houghton Mifflin Reading (2003)
Reading Street (Scott Foresman, 2006)

Textbooks

Super Study Skills by Laurie Rozakis (Scholastic)
Science Explorer (Prentice-Hall)
Social Studies: Regions and Resources (Silver Burdett Ginn)

Fluency Assessments

Procedures and Forms

Don't Speed. READ!

Fluency Assessments: Procedures

Observation

ADMINISTERING

1. Think of a specific question you want to use to guide your observation. Sample questions pertaining to fluency include:
   - How does the child pace the reading of the text?
   - Does the reader understand how to use prosodic features (phrasing, expression, intonation) when reading?
   - Does the reader read at an appropriate rate, with accuracy and prosody?
   - How well can the child retell what was read?
2. Reproduce the Class Observation form shown on page 105.
3. Write the question in the space provided.
4. Write students' names in the left column.
5. Write notes to yourself in the space provided as you observe individual children.

SCORING

There really is no way to score your observations but your notes can shed light on instruction. Analyze your notes to determine whether children were able to perform the reading skill you were observing, and use the results to plan for meaningful instruction.

Running Record

ADMINISTERING

1. Choose a text or passage.
2. Make copies of both the Running Record and the Running Record Summary forms (pages 106–107).
3. Assess children individually. Begin by saying something such as this: "I would like to listen to you read this book. While you are reading, I am going to take some notes so that I can remember how well you read." Sit next to the child so that you can watch his or her behaviors rather than the reverse!
4. Have the child read the book while you record the reading on the Running Record form. Use the following notations:
   - Make a check for each word read as shown in the book.
   - Write and circle any word that is omitted.
   - Add a caret for any word that the child inserts and write the word.
   - Write and draw a line through any word that is substituted and write what the child said in its place.

Fluency Assessments: Procedures

- If the child repeats, draw an arrow to indicate where the child went back to reread.
- Write *SC* when the child self-corrects.

5. To check comprehension, have the child do a retelling (see the Retelling Evaluation on page 103).

SCORING

1. Write M, S, V for each miscue and self-correction in the appropriate column shown on the form. Remember that a self-correction is not counted as a miscue. Likewise, a repetition is not counted as a miscue.
2. Read the sentence up to where each miscue was made and ask yourself these questions:
   - Does it make sense? If so, circle the *M*.
   - Does it sound right? If so, circle the *S*.
   - Does it look like the actual word in the text? If so, circle the *V*.
3. For each self-correction, you need to ask yourself what made the reader go back to self-correct. Ask yourself these questions:
   - Did the child self-correct because meaning was disrupted? If so, circle the *M*.
   - Did the child self-correct because it didn't sound right? If so, circle the *S*.
   - Did the child self-correct because the word didn't look like the one shown in the text? If so, circle the *V*.
4. Calculate the accuracy rate and self-correction rate using the formula shown on the Running Record Summary form.
5. Record additional observations on the Running Record Summary form.
6. Use the results to plan for meaningful instruction.

Modified Miscue Analysis

ADMINISTERING

1. Choose a text that contains 50 to 100 words.
2. Make a copy for the child to read from and have another for yourself. You will make your markings on this copy.
3. Assess children individually. Begin by saying something such as this: "I would like to listen to you read this text. While you are reading, I am going to take some notes so that I can remember how well you read." Sit next to the child so that you can watch his or her behaviors rather than the reverse!
4. As the child reads, make the following notations on your copy of the passage:
   - Circle any word that the child omits.
   - Add a caret for any word that the child inserts and write the inserted word.

Don't Speed. READ!

Fluency Assessments: Procedures

- Draw a line through any word that the child substitutes with a new word. Write the substituted word above the original word.
- Write a *C* on top of the word if the child self-corrects.
- Note repetitions by writing *R* and drawing a line back to where the child repeats.

5. To check comprehension, have the child do a retelling (see the Retelling Evaluation below).

SCORING

1. Using the Modified Miscue Analysis form on page 108, analyze the child's miscues. Here's how:
    - Write each miscue in the Student column and the actual text in the Text column. Remember that self-corrections and repetitions are not counted as miscues.
    - For each miscue, ask the three questions shown on the form and circle the appropriate letter.
2. Use this analysis and the markings on the passage to complete the Summary of Observation form on page 109.
3. Based on your analysis, determine what you think the child needs to learn, and design instruction accordingly.

Retelling Evaluation

ADMINISTERING

1. Make a copy of the Retelling form on page 110 or use it to design one of your own. In either case, read the form carefully so that you will know exactly what to listen for.
2. Select a text for the child to read.
3. Ask the child to read the text.
4. Once the child has finished reading, have him or her do a retell. Say something such as "Tell me everything you can remember about this passage. Pretend you are telling it to a person who has not read it."
5. As the child retells, use the form to record what you hear. You can use prompts such as "What comes next?" or "Anything else?"

SCORING

1. Look at your markings.
2. Make any notes in the Interpretation section at the bottom of the form.
3. Use this analysis when planning instruction.

Fluency Assessments: Procedures

Holistic Oral Reading Fluency Rating

ADMINISTERING

1. Choose a passage or section of a book.
2. Make a copy of the passage for the student. You will make notations on this copy as the child reads from the actual text.
3. Make a copy of the Holistic Oral Reading Fluency Scale on page 111.
4. Read through the scale to determine what you are rating.
5. Show the passage to the child and allow him or her time to practice reading it silently at least once.
6. Ask the child to read the passage orally.
7. As the child reads, mark phrasing by placing slash marks between the words. You may want to record other observations as well.

SCORING

1. After the child has finished reading, have him or her retell the passage or story. How well did the child retell? You may want to refer to the Retelling Evaluation on page 103.
2. Use the Holistic Oral Reading Fluency Scale to rate the student. Circle the number in front of the description that best describes the child's reading.
3. Attach the passage you marked to the fluency scale.
4. Use the child's performance to design appropriate instruction.

Independent Silent Reading Evaluation

ADMINISTERING

1. Reproduce the Independent Silent Reading Log form on page 112.
2. Instruct students to record what they read including the date, title, and a brief evaluation of the text or something they learned by reading the text.

SCORING

1. Periodically, collect the students' reading logs and analyze what you see. For example, you might consider the following:
    - What kinds of texts are the children reading? Are they reading a variety of texts or are they limited in their selections?
    - How long is it taking children to read a given text? Do they stay with a text once they start it or do they abandon it?
    - What kinds of comments are students making about the texts they are reading?
2. Use the answers to your questions to design meaningful instruction.

Fluency Assessments: Forms

CLASS OBSERVATION

Focal question _____ Date _____

Name of Student	Notes

Fluency Assessments: Forms

RUNNING RECORD

Name _____ Date _____

Title of Book _____ Author _____

Page	Reading Performance	Miscues M S V	Self-Corrects M S V
	TOTALS		

M = Meaning Cue   S = Structure Cue   V = Visual Cue

Source: Opitz, Michael F. (1998). *Flexible grouping in reading.* New York: Scholastic.

Fluency Assessments: Forms

RUNNING RECORD SUMMARY

Name _____ Date _____

Title of Book _____ Author _____

Summary of Reading Performance

Total # of Words _____   Total # of Miscues _____   % of Accuracy _____

Reading Level (Circle the one that matches the % of accuracy.)

95%–100% = Independent   90%–94% = Instructional   89% or lower = Frustration

Total # of Self-Corrections _____   Self-Correction rate 1: _____

NOTE: Self-correction rates of 1:3, 1:4, or 1:5 are good. Each ratio shows that the reader is attending to discrepancies when reading.

- -

Summary of Observation

1. What did the reader do when unknown words were encountered?

   _____ made an attempt

   The reader made an attempt in these ways:

   _____ used meaning cues   _____ made repeated tries   _____ used memory

   _____ used structure cues (syntax)   _____ looked at pictures   _____ looked at another source

   _____ used letter/sound cues   _____ skipped it and read on   _____ asked for help

   _____ waited for teacher help   _____ other: _____

2. How often did the reader attempt to self-correct when meaning was not maintained? (Circle one.)

   always   frequently   sometimes   seldom   never

3. When the reader did self-correct, which cues were used? (Check all that apply.)

   _____ letter/sound knowledge (visual)   _____ meaning   _____ syntax (structure)

Calculating Accuracy Rate

1. Subtract the total number of miscues from the total number of words in the text to determine the number of words that were correctly read.

2. Divide the number of words correctly read by the number of words in the passage to determine % of accuracy.

EXAMPLE: 58 total words – 12 miscues = 46 words read correctly

46 words read correctly ÷ 58 total words = 79% accuracy

Calculating Self-Correction Rate

Use this formula: $\dfrac{\text{self-correction + miscues}}{\text{self-corrections}}$ = 1: _____

Source: Opitz, Michael F. (1998). *Flexible grouping in reading.* New York: Scholastic. Adapted from Clay (1993) and Morrison (1994).

Fluency Assessments: Forms

MODIFIED MISCUE ANALYSIS

Reader's Name _____ Grade _____

Title and Pages _____ Date _____

Three important questions to ask for each miscue:
  M = meaning: Does the miscue make sense?
  S = structure: Does the sentence sound right?
  V = visual: Does the miscue resemble the printed word?

Student	Text	Cues Used
		M S V
		M S V
		M S V
		M S V
		M S V
		M S V
		M S V
		M S V
		M S V
		M S V
		M S V
		M S V
		M S V
		M S V
		M S V
		M S V
		M S V
		M S V
		M S V
		M S V

Source: Opitz, M. F. and Rasinski, T. V. (1998). *Good-bye round robin*. Portsmouth, NH: Heinemann. Adapted from Fiderer, (1995). *Practical assessments for literature-based reading classrooms*. New York: Scholastic.

Fluency Assessments: Forms

SUMMARY OF OBSERVATION

Name _____ Date _____

1. What did the reader do when unknown words were encountered? (Check all that apply.)

    _____ made an attempt in these ways:

    ____ used meaning cues   ____ made repeated tries

    ____ used memory   ____ used structure cues (syntax)

    ____ looked at pictures   ____ looked at another source

    ____ used letter/sound cues   ____ skipped it and read on

    ____ asked for help   ____ waited for teacher help

    ____ other: _____

2. Which cues did the reader use most often? _____

    _____

3. How often did the reader attempt to self-correct when meaning was not maintained? (Circle one.)

    always   frequently   sometimes   seldom   never

4. How often did the reader make repetitions? (Circle one.)

    always   frequently   sometimes   seldom   never

5. Did the reader read fluently?

    _____ mostly   _____ somewhat   _____ little

    Comments: _____

6. Did the reader attend to punctuation?

    _____ mostly   _____ somewhat   _____ little

    Comments: _____

Comprehension

Retelling was (Circle one):   outstanding   adequate   inadequate

Comments: _____

_____

Other observations: _____

_____

Source: Opitz, M. F. and Rasinski, T. V. (1998). *Good-bye round robin*. Portsmouth, NH: Heinemann. Adapted from Fiderer, A. (1995). *Practical assessments for literature-based reading classrooms*. New York: Scholastic.

Fluency Assessments: Forms

RETELLING

Name _____

Directions: Indicate with a check the extent to which the reader's retelling includes or provides evidence of the following information.

Retelling	None	Low	Moderate	High
1. Includes information directly stated in text.				
2. Includes information inferred directly or indirectly from text.				
3. Includes what is important to remember from text.				
4. Provides relevant content and concepts.				
5. Indicates attempt to connect background knowledge to text information.				
6. Indicates attempt to make summary statements or generalizations based on text that can be applied to the real world.				
7. Indicates highly individualistic and creative impressions of or reactions to the real world.				
8. Indicates effective involvement with the text.				
9. Demonstrates appropriate use of language (vocabulary, sentence structure, language conventions).				
10. Indicates ability to organize or compose the retelling.				
11. Demonstrates sense of audience or purpose.				
12. Indicates control of the mechanics of speaking or writing.				

Interpretation: Items 1–4 indicate the reader's comprehension of textual information; items 5–8 indicate megacognitive awareness, strategy use, and involvement with text; items 9–12 indicate facility with language and language development.

Source: Opitz, Michael F. (1998). *Flexible grouping in reading.* New York: Scholastic. Adapted from Irwin, P. A. and Mitchell, J. N.

Fluency Assessments: Forms

HOLISTIC ORAL READING FLUENCY SCALE

Level 4   Reads primarily in larger, meaningful phrase groups. Although some regressions, repetitions, and deviations from text may be present, these do not detract from the overall structure of the story. Preservation of the author's syntax is consistent. Some or most of the story is read with expressive interpretation.

Level 3   Reads primarily in three-or-four-word phrase groups. Some small groupings may be present. However, the majority of the phrasing seems appropriate and reserves the syntax of the author. Little or no expression interpretation is present.

Level 2   Reads primarily in two-word phrases with some three-or-four word groupings. Some word-by-word reading may be present. Word groupings may seem awkward and unrelated to larger context of sentence or passage.

Level 1   Reads primarily word by word. Occasional two-word or three-word phrases may occur—but these are infrequent and/or they do not preserve meaningful syntax.

Source: Adapted from Johns, J. L. and Berglund, R. L. (2006). *Fluency: Strategies & assessments* (3rd ed.) Dubuque, IA: Kendall/Hunt.

U.S. Department of Education, National Center for Education Statistics (1995). *Listening to children read aloud, 15*. Washington, DC: U.S. Department of Education.

Fluency Assessments: Forms

INDEPENDENT SILENT READING LOG

Name_____

Date	Reading Material	Overall Response

Explanations of Fluency Activities

Page	Activity Class	Whole Group	Small Group	Partner	Individual	Comb.
114	Read-Aloud	•				
114	Shared Book Experience	•				
115	Echo Reading	•	•			
116	Choral Reading	•	•			
116	Oral Recitation Lesson	•			•	•
117	Fluency-Oriented Reading Lesson	•		•	•	•
118	Partner Reading			•		
119	Readers Theater		•		•	•
120	Cross-Age Reading			•		
120	Poetry Club	•	•		•	
121	Read Around		•			
122	Guess the Emotion	•	•			
123	Cut Apart	•	•		•	•
124	Say It Like the Character	•	•		•	
124	Neurological Impress				•	
125	Reading While Listening	•	•	•		
126	Closed-Captioned Television	•	•			

Fluency Activities

Read-Aloud

Teacher selects and practices a book to read aloud with specific emphases in mind.

- Select a text to share with your students. Choose a passage that you enjoy, one that you think your students will enjoy as well.

- With fluency in mind, set a purpose for sharing the text with your children.

- Practice reading the text before reading it to your students in order to provide a powerful fluency model. It is important that you read in a manner that is appropriate to the type of text you are reading.

- It is helpful to establish a daily routine for your Read-Aloud. You may decide to designate a prepared part of the room for it. Try to make it comfortable and set a mood for the activity. A carpeted area glowing under a soft table lamp is a possibility.

- Be sure to set the stage for the reading and instruct students to pay attention to the meaning as well as the manner in which the text is read.

- Read the text aloud to the students as they listen.

- Model the fluency behaviors appropriate to your purpose for reading.

- Check for listening comprehension and understanding of the fluency components through a discussion following the reading.

Shared Book Experience

Students are seated in front of a big book. After a focused introduction and a first read by the teacher, students chime in on a second reading.

- Choose a big book that meets the fluency needs of the group.

- Set a purpose for the shared reading.

- Invite the students to gather in a small area within view of the print in the big book.

- Introduce the book by pointing to and reading the title, the author's name, and the illustrator's name. You may briefly introduce a character or a small portion of the events so that students can connect with and anticipate the story. Have students predict what they think the book might be about.

Fluency Activities

- Encourage students to pay attention to the meaning as well as the manner in which the text is read.

- Read the text aloud to the students as they listen. Point to the words as they are read in order to demonstrate that the written words convey meaning. Use this opportunity to point out word groupings and punctuation that help you to read in a fluent manner (using reading rate, expression, and accuracy).

- Read the text again and stop occasionally to point out how your manner of reading changes according to the meaning or features of the text (e.g., dialogue or rising action).

- Reread the text several times over several days. Invite students to read along if they wish. As students become more proficient with the text, allow individual students to read. Keep the text on display throughout the school day so that students can read it on their own.

- Encourage students to talk about the story throughout the day—likes, dislikes, funny parts, connections, fluency's role in the reading.

- Provide smaller versions of the text for students to read on their own and even take home if they wish.

- Even after the book has been replaced with another shared book, return to it occasionally for rereading. This conveys to the students that good books are meant to be read and enjoyed more than once! It will also give them a chance to compare the role fluency plays in the reading of different texts.

Echo Reading

The teacher reads a segment of text aloud while students follow along. Then students reread the same segment in unison.

- Choose a text that is appropriate for the reading level of your students. It can be a big book or you can distribute a copy to each child. With a big book, gather the children within reading range of the text that you are using.

- Set a purpose for this fluency activity.

- Read a segment of the text aloud to students. Then point out the text-specific reading rate you used, the way that you emphasized certain phrases, or voiced

Fluency Activities

emotion in relation to the author's purpose (e.g., in anticipation of a climactic event).

• Discuss how the reader knows which phrases to emphasize and what rate of reading to use.

• Reread the text segment again and have students echo your reading after you have stopped reading.

• Continue trading turns in this manner as long as students are successfully mimicking your fluent reading.

• You may need to stop to discuss a specific component of fluency used during reading to clarify its purpose.

• Move on to other genres and more difficult texts according to your students' success and your fluency skill focus.

Choral Reading

Students read a text in unison.

• Select a text to be read as a group. Poems, predictable books, and ritual texts, such as the Pledge of Allegiance, are excellent choices.

• Be sure that every student can see the text. You can provide a copy to each student, gather around a big book, place a copy on the overhead or LCD projector, or write it on chart paper for all to read.

• Model choral reading by first reading the text aloud to the students. Be sure to discuss with the group how you used fluent reading to express the meaning.

• Read the text chorally several times over several days. Use the opportunity to perform the Choral Reading when visitors come to class.

Oral Recitation Lesson

The teacher reads aloud while students follow along. After discussing the text, the teacher rereads the text, stopping at logical places and students echo back each section of text. Students then read a portion of the text on their own until they feel comfortable with the text. They then read it to others in the group.

Fluency Activities

- Choose a text that meets the fluency needs of the group and is appropriate for their reading levels.

- Be sure that each student has a copy of the selection that you want them to read, either the whole text or a selected passage.

- Read the text aloud to the students.

- Following the reading, examine the story components as well as the portions of the text that elicit the components of fluency. A story map may serve this purpose.

- Read a selection from the story aloud to the students. Students may help you choose one that lends itself beautifully to a specific element of fluency.

- Have your students read the selection aloud chorally with you, until they show that they can successfully read with appropriate rate, accuracy, and expression.

- Pair students and have them read the same selection from the text to each other. Ask them to read the selection in the same manner that you just read it as a group. Remind them and discuss the aspects of fluent reading—using adjustable rates, reading with accuracy, and using proper expression.

- After the students have completed the partner reading, read another selection from the text to them, have them follow it with choral reading and then partner reading as before. Continue modeling and practicing several passages until your purpose for the lesson has been met.

Fluency-Oriented Reading Lesson

The teacher reads a grade-level text aloud, and then the class discusses it. Students then practice reading the text in and out of school and read their part of the text to a partner the following day.

- Choose a text that is at the instructional level of your students.

- Determine a purpose for this fluency activity.

- Provide a copy of the text for each of them.

- Read the text aloud to your students.

- Discuss the meaning of the text and have the students point out how fluent reading enhances that meaning. What does it sound like?

Fluency Activities

- Have students practice reading the text in the manner discussed. They can practice during silent reading in class and at home with their parents.

- The following day, they read that portion of text to a partner during partner reading.

Partner Reading

In some manner, students are paired and they read a text together.

PAIRED READING:
- At the first reading session, the student and the tutor (any proficient reader such as a teacher, an older student, or an age-level peer) agree on meeting times.

- The student chooses the reading material and can change it at any time. Remember that the tutor supports the reader while reading. This added support makes it possible for students to read just about any text of their choosing. And don't forget that interest plays a big part in reading success. We are all more likely to stay with a text if we are truly interested in the topic.

- Always begin by reading together. You may want to use a "one-two-three" signal so that you both know when to start.

- Establish a signal that will indicate when the student wants to read solo. It could be a tap on the shoulder or a nod of the head. When the student signals to read solo, the tutor reinforces the student for taking the risk and continues to offer support throughout the solo reading. Either the student or the tutor may stop at logical points to discuss the meaning of what has been read.

- If a miscue is made, the tutor waits to see if the student self-corrects. If not, and the miscue alters meaning, the tutor points to the word and asks, "What would make sense here?" The student supplies the word or the tutor tells the student the word and resumes reading orally with the student, until the solo signal is given again.

PRACTICE PARTNERS:
- This activity is based on the practice students need to prepare for presenting their passages to the class during their oral reading performance.

- The students practice in pairs with the passages they have already chosen for the upcoming performance. The passages can be poems, favorite portions of texts that they have read, or sections from content area texts that they are interested in.

Fluency Activities

- Students make a copy of their passage in order to provide it to their practice partners. Students need to become familiar with their partner's passage by practicing it as well as their own.

- Provide about 15 minutes a day for them to practice with their partners.

- Each student reads along with his or her partner, providing help when it is needed.

- The partners discuss the manner of their reading and their fluency.

- At the end of the week, the students perform their passages for the class.

Readers Theater

Students rehearse a script and once the group feels prepared, present the play to the class, scripts in hand.

- Select the material that you want the children to read or have them choose their own. The key to a successful Readers Theater experience is to find appropriate texts or scripts—ones that lend themselves to being read aloud. You can find scripts in basal readers and magazines. Many children's books are written in ways that make them perfect for a Readers Theater presentation.

- Give an overview of the text and divide the class into groups, making sure that there are enough members to play all the characters in the script.

- Provide students with time to read their scripts silently. Students will need to practice the scripts both individually and as a group to ensure that they are ready to present their play before an audience. The repeated practice provides students with an opportunity to develop the skills associated with good fluent reading— reading accurately, with proper expression to convey meaning, and at a rate that fluctuates according to the phrasing of the text.

- Have the group perform for the class when they feel that they are ready. These performances can be scheduled throughout the week, or they can all be presented at one time.

- After the group performs, you may have the audience respond to particular parts of the play, addressing meaning and fluency. Here are a couple of response ideas:

Fluency Activities

Provide students with blank pieces of paper and have them draw a scene or a character that they visualized as a result of the description given in the story.

Ask students to discuss the fluency of the play and how it related to the meaning of the story (e.g., "I liked the way that the characters fluctuated their reading speed and volume because I could tell that they were excited or angry").

Cross-Age Reading

Students of different ages are paired for reading. They read the same text.

- Guide your students through the study, practice, and celebration of the components of fluent reading. Partner Reading and Say It Like the Character are a few of the many activities described here that can provide your students with the understanding they need for Cross-Age Reading.

- Teach your students how to select texts that are appropriate for their younger reading partners. They can begin by determining the interests of their reading partners through an interview. Younger students may also choose a text to be read at the next meeting.

- Provide time for your students to practice reading the chosen text. Encourage them to rehearse reading as the characters would, with expression and accuracy, and at an appropriate rate.

- Share ways for your students to involve their partners in the reading by modeling possibilities during your Read-Aloud. Discuss how they can promote a love of reading in their partners. It is important that they match their manner of reading to their audience. Model logical places to stop reading and ask questions.

Poetry Club

After hearing the teacher read some poems and explain why he or she selected them to read aloud, students select their own poems. After practicing, they read them aloud to an interested audience.

- Celebrate poetry with regularity in the classroom. Show students your love of poetry by making sure that it is a part of your classroom decor and library. Have several collections of poetry in your classroom and display a favorite book of poetry in a special place.

Fluency Activities

- After reading aloud several poems to students, tell them that they will have the opportunity to look through the books you have displayed in order to choose their own poems to read to the class. Show students the various titles from which to choose.

- Provide students with time to select and rehearse the poems. If poem selection occurs on Monday, students could spend the remainder of the week practicing their poems in different voices, with different phrasing, and at different rates. They need plenty of practice to get the poem "just right."

- Invite students to sign up to read their poems during Poetry Club, which can be held at a specific time on Friday.

- When Poetry Club time comes around, gather the students in a special area of the classroom and have those who signed up share their poems. Students may want to include information about the poet as well as their reasons for choosing the poem.

Read Around

Students gather around a table to share memorable parts of their reading experiences. In turn, they state the title of their book, provide a brief overview, and read a selected portion aloud to the group.

- Invite students to look back through material that they have read to find at least one favorite sentence, paragraph, or passage that they would like to share with others. You can use a variety of reading materials, including books, magazines, comics, poetry, and famous quotes.

- Once they've selected their passages, have students mark them with a sticky note, note card, or bookmark.

- Provide students with time to rehearse their passages silently. Most will need to practice reading their passages several times.

- Ask for one volunteer to read his or her passage to the group while the other students listen. Rather than calling on students, encourage them to take cues from the other students and share their passage when no one else is reading. Order is not important in this reading activity. Please feel free to join the Read Around and share a favorite passage of your own.

Fluency Activities

- Continue reading until every person who wishes to perform has had his or her opportunity.

- Encourage the students to discuss their reasons for choosing their passages. This will help the students see that there are many ways to choose a passage.

- Discuss the manner in which the passages were read. How did they differ according to the type of text shared or the meaning conveyed by the author?

Guess the Emotion

Students read selected sentences with expression, intonation, phrasing, and attention to punctuation. Their audience attempts to determine the emotion expressed in the reading.

- Create a set of sentence strips or collect appropriate sentences from texts that you and your students are reading. Students can be encouraged to collect the sentences during their individual reading practice.

- Provide students with an opportunity to read each sentence in the manner that best conveys the emotion expressed by the character.

- Have students determine the emotion expressed by each of their sentences and record the emotion words on separate note cards. Use students' words to put together a bank of emotions to aid the student audience as they attempt to identify the emotions conveyed by the readings.

- Have the students gather in a small group.

- Spread the note cards face up on the table in the center of the group.

- A student takes a turn reading a sentence in the manner that was intended, the way that the character would have said it.

- The audience tries to determine the emotion that was conveyed by the reading, referring to the bank of emotions if needed.

- After the emotion has been identified, another student reads a sentence until each student has had a turn.

- As a variation, have students attempt to read their sentence with the emotion listed on the card that they draw from a facedown pile located in the center of the group.

Fluency Activities

Cut Apart

A story is cut up into sections, one for each class member. After practicing, students read their sections in sequence.

- Find an appropriate text for your purpose and the reading ability of your students.

- Photocopy the selection. You may need to adjust the size of the print.

- As you read the selection, look for logical stopping points and mark them.

- Look through the whole selection to make sure that you have created enough parts for each student or small group to have a selection.

- Cut the selection apart, mounting each part on card stock. You may also want to list the author, title, and illustrator on a separate card in order to begin the story.

- Number each part. Even though there may be more text in certain selections, mounting them each on the same size card will ensure that no student feels singled out.

- Explain the procedure. I say something like this: "Today you all get to read part of our story. I have put the different parts on these cards. The number on the card will let you know where your part fits. After I hand out the cards, you will need to practice reading your part silently. You will want to think about the way that you read your part. Fluent reading deals with rate, accuracy, and expression. How will you use fluency to practice reading your part? Practice it as much as you can until you share it with the class. I'll be walking around to help."

- Hand out the cards. At times it will not matter who gets a given card; at other times you may want to give students specific cards in order to ensure their success.

- Seat students in a circle in numerical order. Ask the students to focus on what is happening in the story and the way that fluency helps to enhance it. You may need to provide a brief example here or connect their understanding to a previous fluency experience during Cut Apart. Begin by reading the title and author card. Have students follow in turn.

Fluency Activities

Say It Like the Character

Students read a section of narrative text to themselves and decide how the character would say the text if he or she were present. Students then read the part aloud, trying to sound just like the character.

- Have students choose texts. Tell them to make sure their text includes dialogue.

- Invite students to read their text silently. Inform them that they will be reading the text aloud after they have had ample opportunity to practice.

- Identify a passage from the text that you would like them to practice reading. Have them read it in just the manner that the character would actually speak the part.

- Ask students to read their passages aloud, paying attention to how the character might actually say the words and how the character might actually feel.

- Ask questions such as these: "What emotion were you trying to convey when reading?" "What made you think that you should read it the way you did?" Both of these questions invite students to describe how they connect their own experiences with those of the character.

Neurological Impress

The teacher sits alongside the student and reads into the student's ear as the student reads aloud.

- Select a text that is at the student's independent reading level.

- Set a purpose for the reading. Keep initial sessions brief (several minutes) in order to develop a pattern for fluent reading.

- Discuss the purpose with the student before beginning.

- Connect the reading practice and your purpose to an activity that the student is familiar with (e.g., piano practice strengthens the student's ability to play the piano fluently).

- Tell the student that you will be reading the text together in order to help him or her practice. Encourage the student to pay attention to the purpose for reading and your oral model of fluent reading.

Fluency Activities

- Determine a cue for beginning the reading.

- Begin reading together and direct your reading at the ear of the student. You can lead the voice of the student by reading slightly louder and faster to provide a strong model of fluent reading.

- Point to each word in the text as it is being read. The student may do this when he or she feels comfortable.

- Reread the passage several times until confidence is developed.

- As the student consistently displays fluent reading, you can let the student lead the reading. New material may be attempted at this point.

- Johns and Berglund (2006) suggest using the method several times a week for several months. A trained volunteer could help you provide this activity to many of your students.

Reading While Listening

Students read silently while listening to a proficient reader read the text aloud.

- Select materials that are interesting to your students and at their instructional or independent reading level. If your collection of texts permits, let students choose from a group of appropriate texts.

- Prepare a recording of the text. This can be done by you, a parent volunteer, or a student.

- At the beginning of the recording, express the purpose for the reading, identify the page-turning cues used, and encourage the student to track his reading of each word and phrase with his finger or a bookmark.

- While creating the recording, read the text accurately, at the appropriate rate, and with expression to provide a strong model for fluent reading.

- Tell your student or students that they will be listening to a fluent reading of the text and that they will be reading along silently.

- Let them know that they will have several opportunities to read along with the text and then they will read the text aloud to you. You will be paying close attention to their ability to read accurately, to fluctuate reading rate according to

Fluency Activities

the demands of the text, and to read with expression by emphasizing phrases and dialogue.

- After they've listened to the recording, have them practice the text on their own or with a partner. Remind them to practice the text the way that they heard it read in the recording.

- Have each student read aloud to you in order to check his or her fluency.

Closed-Captioned Television

Students watch—and read—a television show with the sound turned off and the captions turned on.

- Choose a television program or video that is both of interest to the children and a strong model of fluent reading. Pay attention to the speed of the captioning in order to prevent the frustration of your readers.

- Set a purpose for the activity in relation to fluency.

- Position the group so that all the students can see the captioning on the screen.

- Discuss with children the purpose for the activity.

- Tell students that they are going to be watching the show with the sound off and reading aloud the captions on the screen while the sound is turned off. They should try to read the captions the way that they would be spoken on the program.

- Turn the volume off and the captioning on.

- Signal for students to begin reading the captioning aloud.

- Stop occasionally in order to discuss the fluency of the caption reading with respect to the purpose of the activity.

Index

A

Allington, R., 21, 37
assessing reading fluency,
  18–26
  comprehension and, 20
  questions to ask and, 24–26
  See also student self-assessments
assisted fluency activities, 37
Atwell, N., 80

B

basal readers, 54
Berglund, R., 37
Betts, E., 20, 21, 76
Blachowicz, C., 21, 91

C

Cambourne, B., 34–35
chapter books, 48
Cieply, C., 21
Class Observation forms, 77
classroom environment. *See*
  nurturing environments
Clay, M., 42–43
compensatory-encoding theory (C-ET), 13
comprehension, 12–13
  assessing reading fluency
  and, 20
Comprehensive Reading
  Inventory, 21
cyber-texts, 50–51

F

family communication. *See*
  parental involvement
Fargstrup, A., 19, 37
fix-up strategies, 67
fluency
  keeping teaching simple
  and, 89
  reader-based processes and,
  12
  text-based processes and, 12

fluency, defining, 6–10
  comprehension and, 10
  difficulty of, 7–8
  importance of, 6–7
  situational quality of fluency
  and, 9
  teaching reading and, 12–17
fluency, larger reading scheme
  and, 67–75
  showing children how it fits
  and, 67–68
Ford, M., 37

G

Griffith-Ross, D., 13

H

Hale, A., 8
Halliday, M., 34, 36
Harris, A., 23
Harris, T., 21
Hasbrouck, J., 21
Herber, H., 63–64
Hiebert, E., 42

I

independent silent reading,
  76–80
  avoidance behaviors and, 77
  observability and, 76–77
  rules for, 80
  text selection guidelines and,
  77
  time on task and, 77
Independent Silent Reading
  Logs, 77
information books (nonfiction), 46
integrated fluency lessons,
  68–71
  skimming, 71–75
  transparency: Determining
  Importance/Fluency, 69,
  71
  transparency: Skimming, 72

J

Johns, J., 37

K

Karp, M., 20
Kucer, S., 62–63
Kuhn, M., 7, 12–13, 37

L

leveled books, 52–54

M

magazines, 49
Morris, R., 7, 12–13
Moskal, M., 91
multilevel books, 46–47

N

National Assessment of
  Educational Progress
  (NAEP), 12
National Institute of Child
  Health and Human
  Development, *Report of the
  National Reading Panel*, 7
newspapers, 49–50
nonfiction books, 46
nurturing environments,
  57–60
  ability grouping, avoiding
  and, 59
  classroom community and,
  57–58
  cooperative groupings and,
  58
  flexible groupings and, 59
  listening to students and, 60
  small groups and, 58
  student involvement and, 58

O

Oliver, R., 8
Opitz, M., 37
oral language, 34